Creating Motivated Kids

Also by Jean Robb and Hilary Letts

Enjoy Your Teenagers

Creating Motivated Kids

Jean Robb and Hilary Letts

HELP YOURSELF

British Library Cataloguing in Publication Data
A record for this book is available from the British Library

ISBN 0 340 78729 5

Typeset by Avon Dataset Ltd, Bidford-on-Avon, Warks

Printed and bound in Great Britain by
Bookmarque Ltd, Croydon, Surrey

The paper and board used in this paperback are natural recyclable products
made from wood grown in sustainable forests. The manufacturing processes
conform to the environmental regulations of the country of origin.

Hodder & Stoughton
A Division of Hodder Headline Ltd
338 Euston Road
London NW1 3BH
www.madaboutbooks.com

To Samantha, Katie, Nathan and their very special family.

Contents

Introduction   1

1   Helping the child who can't be bothered   9
2   Helping the child who is scared of getting it wrong   19
3   Helping the child who won't have a go   30
4   Helping the child who has lost his confidence and
    enthusiasm   41
5   Helping the child who thinks he is no good   57
6   Helping the child who thinks it doesn't matter   71
7   Helping the child who doesn't want to grow up   83
8   Helping the child who has lost his spark   101
9   Helping the child who gives up   111
10   Helping the child who won't work with you   124
11   Organisational skills for children   149
12   Social skills   160
13   Home tuition   184
14   Rewards, bribes and incentives   193
15   Letting go   199

Motivation and Family Groups   206
Index   208

Introduction

This book is for parents and carers who want to encourage their children to take up opportunities, to enjoy a sense of achievement, and to look forward to the next challenge. It is for those who want to help their children to be motivated.

We work with children of all ages and abilities, alongside their parents and carers. Over recent years, parents have become alarmed and worried by a lack of motivation in their children. Parents know that their children need to realise that it is by their own efforts that they will make a difference to their own lives. Parents know that their children need to be motivated.

Children don't seem to know how to stretch themselves and thus discover new ways of enjoying life in the twenty-first century.

Parents want to know how to help their children become motivated.

This book is for parents who want:

- To be supportive parents, not pushy parents
- Their children to have as many opportunities as possible
- Their children to be optimistic

- Their children to be relaxed
- Their children to be motivated

Motivation matters

If you are interested in motivating children in the modern world, this book is for you. This book will help parents and carers of children between the ages of 0 to 16+.

If you are concerned that your children don't seem to be making the most of their lives, this book will have suggestions for you. If other people are saying to you that your children seem to be underachieving, this book will help you guide them towards reaching their potential. If you are a parent who is frightened to let your children deal with life independently, this book will give you the confidence to let them explore.

You can create motivated children. This book will show *you* how.

Motivated children:

- Have the desire to learn
- Give it a go
- Want to see how far they can take something
- Know that having a go is better than hanging back
- Are confident they can think things through

Motivation is the desire to move, the enthusiasm to make a change, and the determination to find some way to start.

In the beginning

Babies have an enthusiasm for life. They delight in what is around them; trying to touch it, smile at it, eat it or see what happens when they drop it. They have a desire to explore, make friends and develop their skills and strength. If you put a baby down it will roll or crawl or toddle to find out more.

How does the motivation bubble burst?

The urge to see what is around us seems so fundamental that one wonders how any child who started like this could turn into a lethargic and defeated individual who 'can't be bothered'. Could it be these children are confused? Maybe they are frightened. Possibly they feel overwhelmed . . .

This is a book with sensible suggestions, even-handed encouragement and practical possibilities for developing children's self-esteem and confidence in their own abilities. It will develop parents' self-esteem and confidence in their own abilities as well. When parents and carers feel confident, capable and competent their self-esteem is assured. They are in a position to take up opportunities. They are motivated.

Motivation in the adult world

There is a whole host of things that we could all do, but don't do because we can't motivate ourselves. There is another whole host of things that we could do, don't want to do, but manage to find a way of encouraging ourselves in order to get those things done. We motivate ourselves.

Some motivation comes from inside us

Motivation comes from what we think:

- Is possible
- Is reasonable
- We can do
- We should do

Some motivation comes from outside us

Motivation comes from what we think:

- We might get
- We might lose

Most of us would like to be able to motivate ourselves to do more than we do at the moment. We think about how much better our lives could be if we were fit, and we vow to get up earlier in order to do some exercise before work; we imagine how beautiful our garden could look and promise ourselves that we will keep up with the weeding; we decide to get our money's worth from our computer and plan how we will learn about all the facilities we could use.

Reward

We motivate ourselves by thinking of the reward: our lives will be better, our gardens will be beautiful, we will get our money's worth from the computer. So then what happens?

Sometimes our motivation works. We are on a roll. Everything seems possible. We start to look around for other ways to improve our lives. Sometimes our motivation seems to disappear. We persuade ourselves that it is better to have an extra half an hour in bed, the wildlife garden is more fashionable than one with tidy borders, or it is not healthy to spend so much time at the computer. If only we could find the motivation that works every time.

Is there a way to motivate ourselves every time?

The answer is no, because we are human. Being human means we have more desires than we have the time, the money or the energy to fulfil. What we *can* do is become better at motivating ourselves to do some things, not all things.

In order to do this, we need to keep a running check on what our responsibilities are. Our responsibilities will change. We will need to notice that they have changed. We will need to notice *how* they have changed. We will need to be motivated to work out how to cope with the change.

The secret of success is to make sure that we have motivated ourselves to do the things that have to be done.

Motivation and you

What are the things that you have to do that you would much
rather you didn't have to do?

- Go to parents' evenings
- Do the ironing
- Write a report
- Defrost the fridge
- Sort out the toys
- Clean the windows
- Sort out your money
- Pay the bills
- Entertain relatives
- Make an appointment
- Check the gutters and drains

What motivates you?

Think back over the last week and see if you can list five things
that you had to do but didn't want to do.

Now write down what it was that got you to do each thing in
the end:

- Desire
- Fear
- Money
- Interest
- Fascination
- Anger
- Love
- Dignity
- Need
- Ambition
- Peer pressure
- Companionship
- Greed
- Laziness

- Jealousy
- Pleasure
- Shame

Is a pattern emerging? It is important that, if you want to help children become motivated, you understand a bit about what motivates you.

Most people are motivated by something. Few people are not motivated at all. The level of motivation may not be very strong but it will be there.

You may not like what triggers you into action but it is better if you can try and understand what motivates you.

Maintain your motivation

Motivation can be precarious. You just get yourself going when suddenly you find yourself stopping. Understanding what demotivates you is as important as knowing what motivates you, and understanding what demotivates you will also help you to spot when your motivation is under threat. Otherwise, you will find yourself losing motivation without knowing why. When you know what demotivates you, you can make small adjustments to protect your motivation.

What stops you feeling motivated?

- Boredom
- Futility
- Deciding that something is too hard
- Lack of space
- Lack of time
- Lack of materials
- Lack of ideas
- Lack of support
- Confusion
- Tiredness
- Other things that need doing
- Jealousy

- Not seeing how something will make a difference
- Not wanting to take a risk
- Not wanting to put the effort in
- Not knowing how to do it
- Resentment that:
  you are not really involved; that someone else is doing it all; that you are only doing it because someone else wants you to do it; that someone else is doing all the best bits; that someone else will wreck it before or after you get it finished; that it was someone else's idea; that someone else will get the praise
- Not being praised
- Not being rewarded
- Not being the best
- Feeling that what needs doing isn't worth doing
- Feeling used
- Feeling unappreciated

With a list as long as this it's a wonder you ever manage to maintain your motivation. So . . .

What keeps you motivated?
At some point in the task you may feel rewarded for the effort you have put in. Your reward may be a feeling of:

- Delight
- Satisfaction
- Relief
- Pride
- Involvement
- Content
- Safety
- Being prepared
- Equilibrium
- Pleasure
- Being honourable

- Being reliable
- Being respected

Keeping motivated is great when it happens. The good feelings that you get as you keep on task carry you through until you have finished everything you needed to do. But that does not always happen. Sometimes, the reasons you find to stop are so strong that you do give up. So what do you do when this happens? Do you have ways to get yourself going again? If you find it hard to restart once you have hit a difficulty, you need to work out what it was that caused you to stop. Was it something physical? If it was, then you may be able to get back on task as soon as you have sorted it out. Was it something emotional? If so, you might need to remember how you have remotivated yourself before. You can overcome the demotivation by letting yourself feel whatever emotions are going through you and then letting them pass. Don't hold on to the emotions as an excuse never to get going again. Was it something beyond your control? If it was, then you have to decide whether it is something you can get into your control, or get somebody else to sort out. Was it something that was too hard for you to do? If so, perhaps you could ask for help, more instructions, extra training or find more information on it yourself.

Making motivation work – the fundamental points to remember:

- Stay optimistic
- Make decisions
- Don't let yourself be overwhelmed by a setback
- Recognise and use the resources you have

Now you know how to do it for yourself let's work out how you can help the kids!

1

Helping the child who can't be bothered

What makes children feel as if they can't be bothered?

- Older brothers and sisters who put them down
- Illness
- Bad teaching or learning experiences
- Lack of self-esteem
- Exhaustion
- Thinking that nothing they do will make a difference
- Depression
- Other people accepting low levels of performance from them rather than encouraging them to set high standards

The girl whose learning didn't fit her

Tessa was a bright little girl. Her parents were high achievers and had very busy lives. Tessa had grandparents and aunts and uncles with whom she spent time, and she also had her own childminder who picked her up from school and looked after her until she either went to her grandparents or her parents came home.

Tessa was a happy and stable little girl. She was able to play with other children happily and generously. Her life was full of activities into which she fitted easily. She was a pleasure to be with.

I hate homework

There was just one blot on Tessa's landscape and that was homework. She had homework from everywhere. There was daily homework from school and she also had tuition in English and Maths, which meant she was expected to spend at least half an hour a day keeping up with the work set. The work was quite repetitive, not fulfilling, and it made Tessa feel frustrated. She began to rebel and argue about whether she was going to do the homework. Homework which she could have done in ten to twenty minutes ended up taking more than an hour.

Everyone coped with the arguments at home until the day Tessa's school complained that Tessa was now doing less work than other children. Her mum was surprised because she knew how bright Tessa was. She had a chat with Tessa. She explained to her that she couldn't understand what was happening. She couldn't understand why a little girl who could do the work easily didn't just get on with it. She had looked at the workbooks and they seemed so simple. Surely it would be easier for Tessa if she just got the work out of the way. The work wasn't hard for Tessa, so why was she trying to avoid it?

Is it all too much?

Someone looking on from the outside might think that Tessa was doing too much. Tessa did have a hectic schedule, but the clubs and classes which Tessa went to outside school gave her a great deal. They provided her with friendships, experiences, contact with interested adults, and confidence in her place in the world and her ability to cope with any situation. Tessa was an only child who lived in a remote place. Her parents worked long hours so they had built up a timetable which meant Tessa could meet up with children outside school and have a varied life.

10

Is it all too hard?

Someone looking on from the outside might think that the work was too hard and that was why Tessa was rebelling. In fact, the work was too easy. It wasn't interesting to her. Tessa was doing it in the most slapdash way possible. She was arguing about whether she had to do it or not because it seemed such a waste of time to her. When she was finally convinced that the work had to be done she would rush at it, make a mess of it, but get it finished.

Is it all too boring?

Tessa's homework was boring and Tessa's only way of making it interesting was to build in a battle about whether she was going to do it at all. Her homework consisted of working through a set number of pages from commercially produced workbooks which are meant to be done by children with very little guidance from adults. Tessa was simply jumping through hoops.

Workbooks

As lesson plans, or as resources for interested and effective teachers, workbooks can be great. Good teachers will use them in their teaching. They won't necessarily go through them page by page, but will pick and choose the bits they know will work and use them at the time they know is best.

Tough for kids

As self-teach books for children working on their own, workbooks can be a disaster educationally: the child can jump through the hoops or fall at the fences and what they discover about their ability to learn can be misleading.

Bright children will find these workbooks easy, because they can use information which is already in their heads. They may think all learning should be as easy as the workbooks and they will not gain the skills for tackling an 'easy' subject to find its depth.

Motivation to demotivation

Children who find these workbooks easy might lose their motivation for tackling something they think is difficult. Children who find these workbooks difficult can feel they are stupid. They may lose their motivation because the questions don't give any guidance for those who can't work out what to do. Children who find these workbooks boring can lose their motivation because they decide that learning isn't interesting or exciting.

It's not what you do, it's the way that you do it

One of the biggest dangers for bright children is the assumption that a clever child will stay motivated if they are given something to do. The truth is a clever child who is not being taught well will become unmotivated. Motivated children, whatever their ability, will become frustrated if they are not taught well. Frustrated children will reject whatever is making them feel frustrated. If children see education as frustrating, they will reject it. On the other hand, if children see education as liberating and involving, they will make it their own.

Helping bright children who have become demotivated

For very bright children who find themselves, like Tessa, uninspired by what they are being asked to do, helping them to become involved in learning again needs careful attention.

They have grown accustomed to using their intelligence to get out of work, and they will build up barriers to what you are trying to do as well. They will be clever enough to make the barrier look like an alternative. They will try to sweep you off your path and on to theirs. They may become miserable and depressed. They may become very excited, so that you feel they have a genuine interest in what you or they are suggesting, but that excitement is short-lived. They might start to feel aggrieved, saying that you are always 'on at them' or are 'on their back'. They will argue that they are able to do the work and so there isn't a problem anyway. They will argue that they still get better marks than some of the other children in the class.

So what can you do?

You have to make it clear to children what the purpose of education is: the purpose of education is to expand the mind, develop a discipline, increase skills and organise thought.

Once a child understands this, then work that is being done can be measured against these criteria.

If the work set by a school is repetitive, then it can be done quickly. This increases their skills. Repetitive work could be made more complex by asking the child how this piece of work could be developed. A bright, motivated child will respond positively to the idea of widening the possibilities once they see the creative potential. The way they decide to widen the possibilities is up to them.

Bright children, wherever their talents lie, can often see things in the abstract, and so their responses to how you make something more complicated can be very creative and unexpected.

How to make even a spelling list interesting to a child who finds it so easy they don't want to bother

Step One – look at the list. The list is:

- Skirt
- Trousers
- Shirt
- Dress
- Shorts
- Socks
- Shoes
- Jumper
- Tie
- Uniform

Step Two – decide how the words in the list can be grouped:

Number of letters
3 – tie
5 – socks, skirt, shoes, shirt, dress
6 – jumper
7 – uniform
8 – trousers

First letter
socks, shirt, shoes etc.

Last letter
skirt, shirt etc.

Number of vowels
1 – shirt
2 – tie

Verbs, nouns, adjectives etc.
The words in this list are all nouns, but can 'tie' be anything else?
What about skirt? Think about dress.

Step Three – find ways of using the words in the list:

As a title of a book or story
The Hamster Ate My Tie
The Trousers that Changed the World
The Mystery of the Disappearing Socks
Harry Potter and the Stranger's Skirt
Tracey Beaker and the Worst Uniform in the World

As the words to a song or a nursery rhyme

> The last time I saw my shirt
> It was talking to my tie.

It made me laugh to see them chat,
It made me wonder why.

As an advert in a fashion magazine
As a rap
As a tongue-twister

Step Four – word analysis:
How many of the words have more than one meaning?
Can you put different endings or beginnings on any of the words?
undress, tied, skirting, shoestring . . . (prefixes, suffixes)

No spelling list needs to be boring again

Even as you read the suggestions we have made, you may have found yourself quarrelling with what we have put in or left out. That is good, because it means you are thinking more widely than we are suggesting. Thinking widely is what you are trying to achieve with a child who finds the set work easy, difficult or boring. You want the child to be:

- Stimulated to want to find out more
- Enthusiastic about the way they can think
- Intrigued by thinking

Stimulate, don't stifle

It is a finely balanced judgement as to what will stimulate creative juices and what will stifle them. If you start to take over, no matter how brilliant your ideas, children can feel stifled. You want to make sure that your children can find interest in the homework themselves.

Finding interest is the skill you want to encourage

Finding interest is a lifelong learning skill as well as a skill that will stand children in good stead through their years of schooling.

Children who are bored at school, whatever their academic

ability, probably don't realise they can find interest for themselves. They can learn that every lesson can be made interesting if they think. They will have a positive attitude to what they need to do.

Your children need to know that their thinking can be private. The lesson might be quite rigid and structured, but their thoughts can be free and creative. Life can be rigid and structured at times but, with apologies to William Blake, if you know how to find the world in a grain of sand you hold eternity in the palm of your hand.

Just being alive can be a joy.

The boy who found the joy

Ben was always depressed. He had been since he was seven. For five years he hadn't thought anything was fair and he was upset most of the time with all the people he was with. When he was home he was upset with his family. When he was at school he was upset with the teachers or the other children. He wouldn't do any activities outside school, because the other people would always upset him.

His handwriting was appalling; he cheated whenever he was playing a game; he did the bare minimum of work, and always made it look scruffy to show he really couldn't be bothered.

Ben had become depressed when his parents split up. He wanted his dad back and he wasn't going to be happy until his dad was back. Ben had the difficulty that many children and adults have of believing it is someone else's responsibility to make them happy. If any part of their life is sad then they feel all of their life is sad. It is a form of loyalty to what went before, but it is also destructive. It is a form of bullying where other people are made to feel guilty and powerless because they can't lift the sadness.

Being sad is OK, but it is not everything

Ben needed to know that:

- Feeling sad was OK
- Feeling sad wouldn't bring his dad back
- As well as the moments of sadness in his life he could find good moments if he chose to look for them
- He could learn how to look for the things that were already good
- There are no guarantees for anyone that life will always work out with every detail being just as they want it
- He could learn how to make the little bit that he was responsible for better

How to encourage a depressed child to make an effort

Step One – choose one thing to improve

Ben was encouraged to choose the presentation of his work as something he could improve.

Step Two – find a way to make a small improvement

Ben chose to always write with a sharp pencil or a pen that didn't leak.

Step Three – find a way to help him notice if there is any improvement

I can't see what you see

At first Ben was reluctant to admit to himself or to anyone else that there was any improvement. He acted as if he were indifferent to the improvement that others could see. It was fine for them if they thought some of his writing was good, but he didn't see any difference.

Ben felt more comfortable damning himself than praising himself. It took weeks of asking Ben to identify which word was the most badly written and then of getting him to say, if that was the worst, which was the best.

One day, Ben started to identify the best first without realising that was what he had done. He was starting to see the positive. This was not a complete change and he often needed to identify the worst in whatever he was doing so that he could find the best.

I can see a way out

The most important lesson Ben learned was that, even if he was depressed, he would always know that he had a route out of his depression. He could find the worst and move towards the best. He even began to see the funny side of his way of looking at the world when he felt upset. He had started to see joy where before he could only see sadness.

If you are trying to motivate children who can't be bothered, remember the fundamentals are:

- To get them to think about their own approach to life
- To help them find satisfaction in what they have to do
- To find a positive step, no matter how small
- To give them back a sense that they can manage what they have to do in a way that will interest them

2

Helping the child who is scared of getting it wrong

What does getting it wrong mean?

We can often think that getting something wrong means we have come to an end. We haven't realised that getting something wrong is just a part of the process of getting it right or getting along.

We can often think that getting something wrong is an indication to us that we are not up to the task, but actually it just means we need some more information, resources or time to get it right.

What can make children feel scared about getting it wrong?

- Being mocked by other children
- Being shouted at
- Being criticised
- Being laughed at
- Thinking they have to get it right
- Being worried about letting themselves down
- Being worried they might cry

- Feeling inadequate and not up to the task
- Thinking that getting it wrong is the end of the world
- Believing that they are stupid and that the next thing they do will reveal that stupidity
- Being afraid that they will be dropped down a group, set or class if they don't meet the required standard

Helping children see the importance of getting something wrong

Some children understand that getting something wrong isn't a disaster. When children are interested in learning something they will spend hours having a go: they fail; they have another go; they succeed. Then they try something harder: they fail and then they have another go.

It is that natural instinct for learning, for trying and retrying that children need to tap into when they are feeling scared of getting something wrong.

In the same way as children can cope with the rough and tumble of learning to ride a bike, ride a horse or do a handstand, they need to learn how to cope with the rough and tumble of getting things wrong.

When learning causes stress

Making effort
You feel stressed when you feel that the effort you have put in counts for nothing because of the error you have made or the error that has been spotted by someone else.

You feel less stressed if you know that the value of your effort isn't taken away by your error, or errors, because you will still know more than you did before you made the effort.

Being judged
You feel stressed when you feel that you are going to be rated according to whether you get something right or not.

You feel less stressed if you rate yourself according to your own values: have you tried hard? Did you put in your best effort? Have you learned something new? Are you happy to try again?

Meeting deadlines
You feel stressed when you feel you have to achieve something in a certain time.

You feel less stressed when you have some control over when you will be ready.

Most of the times when you are stressed about learning you will find that the stress has been caused by at least one of the above, if not a mixture of all three.

How to help a child who feels stressed by learning

See what you can do rather than worry about what you can't do
Nicola was terrified of her maths exam. She thought she hadn't done enough work for the exam, and she thought that the reason for her lack of preparation was that she had a horse she had to look after. In actual fact, Nicola could have fitted in maths revision around looking after her horse, but she hadn't. She was terrified that she would fail her exam. Since the exam was in a couple of days, Nicola was encouraged to revise the things she could do. She could ignore everything else. She might get a pass if she got high marks for what she could do. If she practised the things she understood she could make sure she would get those right.

Build on your strengths, don't be scared about your weaknesses
Dominic had to give a talk at school. It had to be four minutes long, and he could choose his own topic. It had to be interesting enough to keep other people's attention. At first, Dominic was scared stiff at the idea of trying to keep people interested. He thought he would have to choose an extraordinary topic. He

wanted people to be interested and he wanted people to know that he was someone who knew about extraordinary things. He came up with a topic and started to do some research, but was constantly overwhelmed with panic at the idea of what he had to do.

Finally, he suggested to his mum that he pretend to be off sick on the day of the talk. She explained that this wouldn't be a good idea, the talk had to be done and he would probably have to do it when he went back in to school anyway. He began to sob and wail that there was nothing he could talk about. His mum suggested the holiday they had been on.

Dominic was reluctant. Why would anyone else in his class be interested in listening to that? But as he calmed down and began to remember all the souvenirs that he had brought back the ideas about what he could say formed in his mind. Actually, putting together a talk from his memories of his holidays and the souvenirs he had collected turned out to be quite easy. He forgot the panic he had been in and even started to look forward to what he was going to do.

Too scared to put pen to paper

Lots of children feel scared when it comes to writing things down. You can spot children who are scared about writing. They:

- Drop their pencils
- Tell you they are about to start, sharpen all the pencils in their pencil case including the gold and silver ones, and then do absolutely nothing
- Stare into space, telling you they are thinking
- Write two words then rub them out
- Wander around trying to find the bottle of Tippex which they then shake with such enthusiasm that the top flies off and blobs of Tippex end up on the carpet

It's so complicated

Children who enjoy telling stories can find getting the story in sequence a minefield when they have to write it down. Choosing the right words, spelling the words correctly, and writing sentences that make grammatical sense, is so alarming that they would rather not try.

The boy who learned the art of writing a story

Lawrence had a great imagination and a very subtle sense of humour. He loved thinking about stories and telling stories but when it came to writing his story down he froze. When he was telling the story he could develop it logically but when he started to write he felt that he was taking too long. Because he couldn't see the end of the story, he gave up at the beginning.

It was explained to Lawrence that all writers have to plan and replan what they are writing. He began to realise that:

- He didn't have to write his story as fast as he could tell it
- If he read back over his work as he was writing he could keep adjusting it
- If he adjusted it, it would make sense and be the story he wanted it to be

Lawrence had a go and found that he could master the technique.

If you have children who can't get going on writing their ideas down there are techniques you can teach which will mean they will feel motivated to become independent writers.

Step One – writing about your own life

Many children can't imagine why anybody else would want to know about their life. To help children like this, get them to tell you something they have done. After some prompting they might tell you that yesterday they went swimming. Ask them what they were doing just before they went swimming. Perhaps they were playing in the garden. Then what were they doing before that.

Were they at school? Don't try to get them to fill in the details, you are merely building up in them a sense that they have a life that is meaningful. They have a life that has continuity and a life that is interesting to others.

You could try writing down the things they can remember as they say them, so that it is a speedy exercise. While they tell you what happened before each thing don't interrupt, even if you know they have missed things out. The reasons for not interrupting are:

• Children need time to think through what they want to say
• You could interrupt their train of thought so that they lose what they were going to say
• You might suggest something that mattered to you and miss out on hearing what mattered to them

If you keep interrupting with your thoughts they will start to give up and the exercise will become, yet again, one where they feel they have nothing to say and you end up feeling frustrated or supplying all the ideas.

Step Two – making up sentences
Often children get homework where they have to make up sentences using the words that they have to learn for their spelling tests. These sentences are meant to show that they understand what the word means and how it can be used. Many children panic at this point because:

• It seems a lot to do
• They don't really know what the words mean
• They can't think of sentences

Dictionaries can help. If children are worried that using a dictionary is cheating, they can look up the word in several dictionaries, close the dictionaries, and then write their own sentence. They will have got some inspiration from the dictionaries but the sentence will be their own.

Children often think that they should be able to do everything out of their own heads, but the only time that this is a requirement is when they are doing a test or an exam, or when they have been told they are to write down what they know without any help.

Mostly homework is a chance to practise, use resources and find out more.

Step Three – comprehension

Make sure children who panic about doing comprehension-type exercises, where they have to read a passage and answer questions on it, know they are allowed to look back at the piece they have read. Often children think they are only allowed to read the piece once and then they should have a snapshot of all the information. They try to answer all the questions by drawing on what they can remember from only one reading and if they can't remember they make it up. They won't get very good marks if they try to do comprehension exercises like this and they will lose all interest as the effort they feel they have put in is not reflected in the marks they get.

You can help by getting children to make up their own questions. Children need to know how to get to grips with a comprehension. They could start by reading the passage and writing down their own questions before they try to answer the questions someone else has given them.

When they are reading and asking questions themselves, they start to see where their questions come from. Since they can decide on their own questions, they will have a more open mind when they come to tackle someone else's questions. They won't think they are going to be tricked by someone else who has made up the questions.

Children could start by making up simple questions, such as what is the character's name? Where does he live, and what time of year is it? Questions where all the answers are straightforward. The questions don't have to be written down, they can just be asked out loud. It makes it easier for children when they realise where questions come from. They start to spot the type of sentences that have questions asked about them, and it makes it easier for them to find answers when they go on to do the actual comprehension.

Step Four – writing book reviews

Unless children understand what goes into a book review, they can find writing one very hard. They may not be sure how to sum up the feelings they had and the experience they had when they read the book. They are often given a structure, but if children don't understand the elements, the structure itself will confuse them rather than be a guide to how to do the review. Included in a book review could be:

- A summary of the story
- Information about the author
- Information about the illustrations
- Whether the book is fact or fiction
- Descriptions of main characters
- The sort of book – its genre – whether it is a family story, a funny story, an adventure story and so on
- Who they would recommend the book to
- How many marks they would give it out of ten
- How it compares to something else they have read
- Whether they would like to see it made into a film or a television series
- Whether they would like to meet the characters
- Which bit they found the funniest, saddest or most frightening
- How long it takes to read
- Whether it is value for money

Children are motivated to write something when they understand how to do it. There is nothing more demotivating than not knowing how to do something and feeling that any effort put in will be wasted.

To get a good mark for a book review it is important to avoid the book review becoming a list, although it is better to have a list than nothing at all. To avoid children writing a mere list of likes and dislikes about the book, try to help them make each sentence start with a different word or phrase. For example:

- I loved . . .
- I found . . .
- I thought . . .
- In the bit about . . .
- When the . . .
- — was the character I liked best because . . .
- My heart was in my mouth when . . .
- I got a bit bored . . .
- I giggled when . . .
- The bit that made me laugh the most was when . . .

The reason that book reviews are so important is that they are the first steps in the art of criticism. Any child who wants to get a reasonable pass in secondary school in English will need to know how to critically analyse a poem, short story, novel, play or article. Knowing what you felt and why you felt it as you were reading or watching gives you a lot to draw on when you have to do some writing. It helps you get into a piece of work written by someone else. You learn how to be objective – talking about what the author was trying to achieve – and subjective – talking about how it affected you.

Step Five – *writing an essay*
Will didn't feel at all motivated when the teacher said that his homework for the week was to write an essay entitled 'Why I Like Football'. The rest of the class were to write essays about their favourite sport as well. Will lived and breathed football, so when his parents heard what he had to do they were pleased. At least this homework wouldn't be a battle.

Will did not seem as keen as they were but then he was only twelve. He sat down and wrote the title. Then he drew a picture.

Then he scowled and then he rewrote the title but this time he did bubble writing. Then he asked his dad if he could scan into the computer some pictures from his football magazines for his essay. As yet, apart from the title, nothing had been written. By this time there was only half an hour left to get the homework done because Will had Scouts, and so he asked his mum for some help because he couldn't think how to get started.

Ways in which Will's mum was able to help him write an essay of reasonable length were:

Keywords

Will needed some keywords about the topic to start with. These could come from books, magazines, brainstorming, newspapers or the computer. He could find them himself. Keywords are words that stimulate you to write something on the topic using that word and will probably lead you to write more once you have got going.

Keywords for football might be names of teams, names of players, words about skills or kit and words about watching or playing football.

Questions

Think of some questions that the essay could answer. Am I a player? Where do I play? Whom do I play for? What am I good at? What successes have I had?

Making good use of notes

Thinking of questions that you can answer can help you avoid simply copying your notes out. It helps you find the detail in your own notes. It brings the notes you have copied off the board or been given as a handout into your control. The handouts and notes are general and now you have to show what happens when you use your mind to make sense of them.

Remember the fundamentals of helping a child who is scared to get it wrong:

- Show them a mistake is an opportunity to learn
- Remind them to find what doesn't frighten them and start on that
- Get them to stop and think of a question they can ask
- Help them see that fear uses up energy which could be better used on what they have to do

3

Helping the child
who won't have a go

Why won't children have a go?

- They don't know how
- They didn't realise they could
- They haven't been encouraged to have a go
- They didn't realise that if they had a go they could work out what to do
- They think that not being picked as the first person to have a go is a personal attack and they won't have a go unless they can be first
- They see having a go as entering into a competition
- They see all of life as a competition and if they are not first they are nowhere
- They are so sensitive that anything that causes them discomfort they see as causing them pain and so they withdraw from having a go

The boy who needed the missing ingredient before he would have a go

Luke was completely unmotivated. He seemed to have lost his drive in most areas of his life. He didn't have any particular hobby, didn't have any particular friends whom he cared about, didn't enjoy any subject at school. This was surprising because it was obvious that Luke had a lovely sense of humour. Adults meeting him for the first time would always comment on what a pleasant boy he was. At family gatherings or parties other children would gravitate to Luke. They seemed to really like him. Luke did not appear to be conscious of this and would never respond to their enthusiasm to have him in the game or involve him in the conversation. He was a watcher and an outsider. It was as though he was sleep-walking through his life. There were never any highs or lows with Luke, just a minimal amount of activity and a minimal interest in what was going on.

There was one other part of Luke's life that was really stopping him from gaining confidence: he was afraid of the dark. He wouldn't go anywhere in the house or outside if it was dark. Although most children are scared of the dark they learn to manage their fear. They may not overcome their fear, but they work out how and when to put on lights, carry a torch or talk themselves through their panic when they are somewhere that is dark. Luke just avoided having to be anywhere on his own when it was dark.

Luke was losing ground

At school, Luke was operating way below his potential. One look at his books showed someone who was indifferent to what was happening in the classroom and indifferent to other people's opinions of him. Work was unfinished and untidy. All the way through Luke's exercise books were requests from Luke's teachers that he go and see them, requests that he talk to them about why work had not been done and requests that he finish things that had been left mid-sentence. No one seemed to be able to break into Luke's apathy. Whenever his parents went to meetings with Luke and his teachers, Luke would sit quietly but be unable to offer any explanations for why he hadn't done something.

Luke had an older brother. He was quite different to Luke. He had high opinions of his own abilities and always felt he could succeed. He and Luke had never had very much to do with each other, they were very different personalities and it wasn't surprising that they kept out of each other's way.

The missing ingredient

Most younger siblings need attention from their older brothers and sisters. As it turned out, Luke was no exception. He was unaware that he wanted his brother to notice him and to care about him. He needed his brother to be interested in his progress and to be proud of him.

It was not until Luke's brother became one of the assistants in the computer club at school that things began to change for Luke. Previously, his brother had had no interest in anyone younger than himself, but now he found he wanted to know about what younger boys were trying to do with their computers. He started to ask Luke questions about computers. As he began to build up some understanding of the needs of boys in the lower years at school he also got to know a bit about Luke. He made opportunities to talk to Luke and showed him some of his ideas about projects that the computer club could tackle. Luke himself did not go to the computer club. He wasn't the sort of pupil who went along to anything on a voluntary basis. If he didn't have to he wasn't going to.

Luke lightens up

As a relationship began to develop between Luke and his brother, Luke's parents started to notice changes. They felt Luke was 'lightening up'. They noticed an energy in his voice and a spring in his step that hadn't been there before. They thought at first that it was because Luke was becoming interested in computers, and they tried to encourage him to go along to the sessions that his brother was helping out at, but Luke was quite adamant that computers weren't his 'thing'.

What was influencing Luke was the contact he was having with his brother. Up until now, Luke had thought that if his own brother didn't find him interesting, then he couldn't be interesting. No one had realised that this was the missing ingredient. The whole household changed. Luke asked his brother questions and his brother answered them. Luke became a more stimulating person to have around. Everyone became more alive as Luke became more involved in what was happening at home. Even his fear of the dark seemed to get better. He was prepared to carry a torch as a way of coping with spaces in the house that previously he would have avoided unless he had company.

Luke's motivation was dependent on his brother's interest in him. His parents and his teachers had been encouraging, they had offered help, praised him when they could, and tried to explain how important it was that he always try his best, but none of this had worked. Once Luke felt his brother was interested, everybody else's interest could build on that.

Making someone matter

Some children need a particular person to take a close interest in them in order for them to thrive.

If you have a child like Luke, see if you can work out who it is that he is waiting to be noticed by. It could be an older brother or sister, it could be a parent, it could be the person at school who is often in the limelight.

Decide whether it is possible to make that person interested in becoming a 'friend'. Their interest has to be real. They need to establish a natural relationship with the child where the child is doing something with them so that the child feels that what they do matters and what they say matters.

The girl who wouldn't have a go unless everyone thought she was the best

Rachel liked to be the centre of attention. She was used to having all her needs met by her extended family. Whatever she did at home was met with squeals of approval. Rachel was used to living in a fast lane of admiration. At home, there were many people who were happy to admire Rachel.

When Rachel went to school, she found being deprived of this sort of admiration intolerable. She tried everything she could to have adults and children gaze in amazement at whatever she had done. No one had told her that school was a different place to home. At school, approval for what you have done is much quieter and comes for particular things. Rachel became more frantic in her attempts to try and get the approval she craved. When she couldn't get it, she would strike out at children who had been praised and be nasty to children who had been told off. She would refuse to join in.

Rachel loses touch
Because Rachel's strengths weren't being noticed, she became very jealous of all the other children and couldn't bear that they didn't want her as the star attraction in their friendship groups or to hear what she had to say in class discussions. She was incapable of making the type of contribution that would mean she was part of the activity. She only wanted to make a contribution that would mean she was leading the activity. She was endlessly motivated to be the star. She was not motivated to be a bit-player.

She couldn't see that her selfishness would lead to an impossible situation for her, and her extended family couldn't see that their behaviour had created the situation.

Helping the star to play on the team

Step One – identify the problem

- Does the child draw attention to himself, regardless of whether it is good attention or bad attention?
- Do you find the child 'sitting out' or appearing to make himself different by refusing to join in with others?
- Do you find the child can't judge the pace or the atmosphere in a group?
- Does the child try and disrupt the group even though he has chosen to be apart from the group?
- Does the child exaggerate the importance of the role he took in anything he has done – 'I told everyone else what to do', 'They all had to copy me because I was the only one who knew what to do'?

Children who set themselves apart like this often don't know how to join in with a group.

Step Two – helping a child to see how to play a part

Getting a child to join in can be a long and slow process because they will be frightened that by joining in with everyone else they will lose their star status. They are frightened they may even reveal that they don't actually know how to do something. Children who want to be the star will probably deny that they don't know what to do which can make helping them tricky. Encourage them to start noticing what other people do and to think of something they could praise someone else for.

Step Three – helping a child to see that even stars need to keep on learning

Children who are always praised for what they can do lose the ability to take on challenges that are set by somebody else. They have been over-praised for small achievements and think that if they don't keep repeating those achievements they won't get praise.

Encourage children to choose one thing that they can't do and see if they can learn how to do it. What this exercise will help them develop is the understanding that they're still worth something even when they are learning. Children who feel they have to be best, and who won't have a go unless they can be, are scared that they will lose their identity if they are seen to be a novice at something.

The girl who couldn't bear to be noticed

Natalie was a frightened little girl. When she was out, she would hide behind her mum and dad. She would only look at the floor. She wouldn't answer anybody who tried to talk to her.

Natalie had been born at the same time as her grandmother was dying. Her grandma had been diagnosed as terminally ill three months before Natalie was born and had died the week after Natalie had arrived. The family were grief-stricken. Natalie's grandma hadn't been very old and hadn't had many illnesses. Her illness had come as a great shock to the family, and so, for the first few months of Natalie's life, her mother and father were still reeling from what had happened.

Family turmoil

What should have been a happy time for Natalie and her parents had in fact been full of trauma. In the last months before Natalie was born, all the talk had been about Natalie's grandma. Trips to the hospital and then the hospice had been upsetting. Natalie was born into a grief-stricken atmosphere. Her mum missed her own mother terribly in the first few months of Natalie's life. It seemed so cruel to her that Natalie would never know her grandma, and it seemed so hard not to have her own mum there to talk to, as she became a mum herself.

Keeping quiet

Natalie had not been a demanding baby. She was quiet and well-behaved. It was as if she sensed the need for her mum and dad to have some peace. As she grew older, her quiet manner and her silent detachment became worrying. When other children would get excited by a bouncy castle at a party, Natalie would have to be coaxed on and would slide off the minute she could. She didn't scream or yell, she just took herself off at every opportunity, or stood at the edge of what was going on.

Natalie seemed to be a shy scaredy-cat. She wouldn't stroke next-door's dog, although she loved watching it out of the window. She wouldn't hand the money for her comic over to the newsagent, although she enjoyed going to fetch it. It was as though Natalie felt safe as long as she was uninvolved. As long as she could pull back from any situation she could cope, but, if she felt trapped, then she would become very stubborn and sometimes cry with fury.

Not joining in

Natalie's mother was going to take a part-time job and needed Natalie to go to the local nursery school two mornings a week. Natalie's parents just couldn't imagine how they were going to get her to cope with nursery. When they mentioned the idea to Natalie they were met by silence.

The staff at the nursery school weren't worried by the fact that Natalie was so quiet. They had had quiet children before who had taken time to settle in and they felt sure that after a few weeks Natalie would find her feet. They were optimistic. At first Natalie would only watch from the outside while she clutched a toy she had brought from home. She refused to sit on the carpet for stories or songs, choosing instead to lie under the table.

The biggest problem at the nursery was that some children started to mimic what Natalie was doing. They would crawl under chairs and tables, toss their heads and ignore the adults. They would giggle in a silly way when they wouldn't have giggled that way before. It became very tiring for the teachers until they made a plan.

Step One – help other children to act as good role models

The teachers at the nursery school re-established the way they wanted the children to behave. They used the skills they wanted Natalie to master as part of 'circle time'. The teachers would say things such as: 'I am looking for someone who is good at folding their arms', or 'Jonathan, can you show me how well you can sit up straight?' The children loved these games.

Show by example

Small children love to show how clever they are. The teachers got lots of opportunities to reinforce the behaviour they wanted and praise the children for the behaviour they needed.

Children who had been unsure about how the teachers wanted them to behave got the chance to look at lots of good models. Natalie got the chance to hear the laughter and the praise. She also got the chance to see how people could join in. At first, she refused to watch. An adult would sit near her but that adult's attention was focused on the group activity.

Stay optimistic

Over a few months, Natalie moved from being an outsider to being an interested spectator. When she was encouraged to join in, she hung her head but didn't move away. Gradually, staff noticed that when someone else was picked to sit up straight or look at the teacher, Natalie was doing it as well. If they praised her she immediately stopped. If they mentioned it later or told her mum when she was being picked up, she would hang her head and become mute.

Although the teachers felt that they might be risking the progress Natalie had already made, they continued to gently encourage Natalie to accept more limelight.

Step Two – make the child's world bigger

Natalie began to make overtures. She would say 'good morning' to one member of staff and show her something she had brought from home. The teacher whom Natalie was happy to talk to would listen to Natalie tell her about her toy and would then catch the eye of another teacher or child and tell them what she had been told by Natalie. This avoided the situation where Natalie was controlling who she would interact with and who she would exclude. Other people were drawn into Natalie's world. Natalie was cross when the teacher involved other people, but the staff never let go of the principle that Natalie needed them to help her feel comfortable with other people.

Natalie's progress wasn't easy to see. It was only when her teachers or her parents noticed that she had suddenly handled a situation sensibly that they realised how much progress she must have been making.

Step Three – help the child make a trade

As Natalie became more at ease in the nursery, the teachers were able to help her understand the trade-off which can come in social relationships. If Natalie decided that she wouldn't join in one activity then the trade-off was that she couldn't join in another activity – whether she wanted to or not. Natalie got better and better at understanding the trade-off, and after just a couple of weeks, it was obvious that she was thinking about the consequences of saying no or refusing to join in. She was joining in most of the time.

Step Four – reward the child with responsibility

As Natalie became more confident about being able to join in, she also became more confident about being someone who could help. Her teachers and parents offered her chances to take responsibility for herself, whether it was for some equipment or for helping another child. Her beaming face when she had done something delighted everyone and Natalie felt pleased that she could have this effect on people.

The fundamentals of helping someone who won't have a go are:

- Remembering that you are helping them see themselves as a *part* of the group and not *apart* from the group
- Giving them chances to join the group, come away and try again
- Believing that they can be motivated to take a risk and have a go
- Believing that their unwillingness is not a part of their personality which will never change

4

Helping the child who has lost his confidence and enthusiasm

The zest for life

Watch a group of children when they arrive at a park. There is a sudden explosion of energy as they race for the space where they can feel free. They pitch themselves headlong into everything around them. Some children race to get to the top of the climbing frame, others boot the ball into the distance and then charge after it, some will swing high and fast, and some will dance around with joy at just being there.

The zest for life oozes from children. They are enthusiastic about what is possible, they are thrilled by what is available, they are excited about what is imaginable. This vitality is infectious. It's great to watch and even more fun to be a part of it. Children who are swept up by the adventure are happy to have others join them. The more the merrier as they try to dig a hole to the other side of the world or build a snowman the size of the house. The real world gets forgotten as everyone joins in with the dream. Adults run about finding odds and ends they think will be useful. It's great to make a contribution. It's great to feel involved.

The zest for life makes children positive about possibilities. Children leap out of bed excited about what they are going to do next. Adults hide under the pillows muttering about respectable times to wake up and the need for eight hours sleep a night, but the kids are raring to go. It's as if children with this zest for life are intoxicated with energy, enthusiasm and excitement.

When children have been ill, their zest for life needs rebuilding.

Helping a child who has been ill and who has lost his confidence or zest for life

What can make children who have been ill lose their confidence and zest for life?

- They haven't got anyone to share their experience with so they feel lonely
- They are generally run down and need rebuilding mentally, physically and spiritually
- They are not sure how to get going again
- Although everyone around them slowed down to help them while they were ill, now that they are better, those people have resumed their own lives
- Everyone else might be going at a totally different pace
- They may be worried that they are going to get sick again

When a child has been ill, it is difficult knowing whether their lethargy is due to left-over problems from the illness, warning signs that the illness is reoccurring, or their own lack of confidence that they are well enough or able enough to join in or catch up.

In order for children who have been ill to regain their confidence, they have to feel part of their own life again. They need to get involved. They need to work out ways of resuming life in a way they can manage. When children are ill, other people step in and take charge of the pace and the content of their lives. Sometimes, they have to sit around a lot waiting for appointments. Sometimes, their illness or injury has meant they have to be still, they can't run around being active.

The temptation can be for some teachers and parents to help children who have been ill try and catch up by giving them extra homework, extra lessons, copying up of notes, background reading and videos to watch. This is particularly the case when there are exams coming up. Everybody may think that the main thing is for the child to try and get the most marks possible. They may think this will happen if the child does as much work as he possibly can. In some situations this might work. It might be more sensible to be selective and make sure the child understands the things he feels confident about rather than overwhelming him with the sense that it is all hopeless and he can never do enough or, in the worst cases, can't do anything.

For other teachers and parents, the temptation can be to take the pressure off. They feel the child has had such a miserable time that he should have some treats.

The temptation can be for children to put pressure on themselves to do just as well as they would have done if they hadn't been off.

The boy who wanted to try

Three weeks into the term, Freddie broke his leg badly. He couldn't go into school and, although he had been sent work to do at home, it had been difficult to organise support so that he could keep up with his classmates. When he went back to school, he tried to make up for lost time. There was to be a test at the end of term. He found he couldn't catch up because the rest of the class were revising things they had been taught while he was off and he couldn't work out how to teach himself these topics.

He felt cut off from his classmates, who were all able to talk about the same things, and he felt cut off from any chance of being able to do the test as well as he could have if he hadn't broken his leg. He began to lose his confidence, and he felt tired all the time.

His parents were sympathetic and told him he should do his best, but that didn't comfort Freddie. It seemed to him that life was unfair. He didn't want to be somebody with lower marks than everyone else in his class. He tried as hard as he could but just couldn't seem to work some things out. He was ready to give up.

His form teacher noticed his distress and suggested that Freddie do a test paper from a previous year to see how much he could do. He didn't need to do the test in test conditions. This was a practice. The aim was to see how many marks Freddie might get so he could have an idea of how well he might do in the real test. Freddie agreed because he thought it was a good idea. Once he had done the practice test, he stopped dreading a low mark. He realised:

- There would be some questions that he would not be able to do
- There would be questions he would be able to do
- The questions he would be able to do would make up about three quarters of the exam
- If he got most of the questions he could do right, he would get more than half marks for the test

Freddie became calm about the exam. He knew more about what would be possible, and he felt he could cope with the situation rather than having to run away from it. He could talk to his parents, friends and teachers about the test without feeling panic-stricken that he was going to do so badly that he would never live it down. He had gone from not having any idea about how much he would be able to do in the exam to knowing roughly how many questions he would be able to answer and how many marks they were worth. He felt that he might be able to get quite a lot of the ones he could do right. He realised the situation was fair and wanted to work to get the best marks possible.

His tiredness turned into energy as he practised what he knew and aimed to get all the questions he tackled right, and his air of tragedy and self-despair was replaced by his normal, positive approach – which meant that his friends, parents and teachers could relax because they knew he was back on track.

Loss of confidence

Children who have missed out can lose their motivation when they are worried about whether they will catch up or be able to find a path back to the activities, friends and fun they had before they were ill. They need help to regain their confidence.

When children have no confidence, they often don't see the point in even starting. They may not be able to start at all. They may have false starts. They may have fumbled starts. They don't feel viable. They don't recognise their resources. They don't feel that this is a place where they should be.

There are many reasons for children who were confident to lose their confidence. It doesn't take much for a child who knew exactly where they had to start and felt confident about starting to feel at sea. They may have been ill. They may have been away. They may have had an upset. Something exciting may have happened that has thrown them off course.

Having confidence

When you have confidence you can see the point. You can see the point in making a start; you can see the point of what you are doing; and you can often see the point where you are going to finish.

Confidence comes from knowing how to make a start, and making a start means marshalling your resources. Your resources are:

- Memory
- Logic
- Maturity
- Patience
- Optimism

- Imagination
- Willingness

I just can't remember

Children who have been ill and lost their confidence haven't been using their memory for the things they now need to remember. When they try and remember something, they can't find it in their memory bank. Their confidence starts to wobble because they are not sure what else they might have forgotten, which they might be expected to know. Even worse, adults can't understand what is happening. Adults can get irritated when children can't seem to remember something and make children so nervous that they find it impossible to remember anything.

Other adults can be over-protective when children find it hard to remember. They step in too early with the information that the child has forgotten, instead of helping the child find a way to remember. They don't give children clues to help them remember. They encourage children to let the adults do the remembering for them.

Rebuilding memory

Often, when children have been ill, they have lost the opportunity to tell the adults with whom they live about what has been happening. The adults don't need to be told because they have been there too. There has been no need for the child to retell a story. This is a change. When children are well, they will often be doing things away from their family. They will be going to school or playing with friends. They will have been out with the youth club or on a trip with other relatives. When they get back, everyone will be interested to hear about where they have been, what they have been doing, who they have been doing it with, why they were doing it and what they were thinking about or learning as they were doing it. The child gets a chance to build up his memory naturally.

Once children have recovered from an illness, you need to give them the chance to retell stories about what has happened to them. They need to be given the chance to draw on their own memories so that they know they can. Get out old photos and look at them together. Look through old school books. Encourage them to watch videos that they have watched before. Look at the badges they got for swimming or the certificates they won at drama. Give your children the chance to reactivate their memories.

It doesn't make any sense

When children start to lose confidence in their memory they can feel that their whole world is falling apart. All their life they have built their own world. They have built a world of understanding based on the memories they have. The parts of this world are held together by their memory. They start to lose confidence or panic when they feel the bits they have forgotten were like the mortar holding the rest of the building together. Now they have forgotten some details it is as if the mortar has disintegrated. They can't see an order to any information, they can't see the logical link between one fact and another, and they stop expecting there to be any logic and start feeling completely muddled. They are stymied until someone can help them reorder the bits and replace the mortar.

Reassembling logic

Jigsaws are an excellent way of helping a child who has been ill and begun to think that there is no logical sequence to anything that happens. Working on jigsaws helps children build up the idea that they can find the order in anything they have to do. Most people who do jigsaws will have a starting point that they feel very comfortable with. They might hunt for the four corners first or sift through to get all the edge pieces.

Having something to do first means that you can:

- Make a start
- Be busy getting on.

- Have a look at, and familiarise yourself with, what you will be working on later without getting into a panic that you have to do something about it now. As you are sorting out all the edge pieces you are noticing the colours, shapes etc. on the other pieces but don't feel under pressure to get them all organised until you have done the edge
- Go at a pace that keeps you calm and purposeful

Practising jigsaws helps children work out logical links between one piece and another. They will then use the same skill to build up logical links between other things they know, other things they have, or other things they have to do.

I've been ill so you can't expect me to do it

It is very hard for a child who has been ill to pick up the reins and take charge of his own life. While he was ill, other people had to take responsibility for him. Now he is better and on his own and very little is familiar, his maturity can collapse under the strain.

Even if children have been ill, they still have to move on. They will be helped but they are now the key players in their own lives. They don't need to be scared about this change, they simply need to take charge of what they can gradually.

One of the most important lessons of growing up is when children learn that they choose the quality of the lives they have. In every situation the choices they make will have an effect on their own self-image. Their own self-image is critical to their developing maturity.

Children show maturity when they can see a situation from another's point of view, judge the pace of the activity and learn from their mistakes. Children need to learn that maturity includes being responsible and trustworthy.

Relocating maturity

Be firm about some things that you do expect children to do once they have recovered. It doesn't really matter if the thing you choose is something quite simple or something that doesn't take very long. The important thing is that you are encouraging such children to 'pick up their own bundle' and expecting that that is what they will do gradually. By starting off gently, you will be getting the message across that you expect them to take some responsibility and get something done. As their energy returns they will take on more. If they are doubtful or frightened about taking up the reins of their old life again, just keep identifying small ways they can take charge. They might not be strong enough to walk to school, and will need you to give them a lift, but they will be able to pack their own bag and maybe carry it to the car.

You are a person in your own right and others have rights too

A lot of children are very patient when they are ill, putting up with things which adults know even they themselves would find difficult to bear. Adults are often surprised at how patient and brave children are.

Some children are very impatient when they are ill, however. They may find the pain too frightening to be able to lie still and wait and their frantic pleas for help create stress for everyone around them.

Children who have been patient through their illness may be so passive when they are no longer ill that no one notices them when they try to take up their old lives. They are relying on someone else sorting out what they need.

Children who have been impatient when they are ill may be very demanding when they take up their lives again and find it very difficult to cope when they feel they are not being helped.

Repositioning patience

Children may need guidance in how to ask someone for help. If they are in a panic, they will often demand help with such urgency that they can sound quite rude. Then they don't understand why the person they have asked to help them is short with them or tells them to go away. Children need to find a way to ask for help that won't put unnecessary pressure on the person they need the help from. Parents can help by role-playing with their children ways of attracting someone's attention and asking for help.

This can be useful too for children who are very passive, quietly sitting in a corner waiting for someone else to notice that they need help. Encourage them to try out different ways of asking for something. Just having an idea of what to say and how to say it can be enough to help quiet, passive children realise that they are able to make a request themselves.

Make sure your child is getting enough sleep because learning how to be a helpful part of a group can be quite demanding.

Daydreams and nightmares

When children have been ill, they can spend a lot of time dreaming about what it will be like when they get back home or back to their old friends or back to their classmates at school. They might have had letters from school and letters from friends to cheer them up and so they might feel as though their place is secure. They might be full of optimism.

Sometimes, children may feel that they will be forgotten by their friends. They may worry that their best friend will have found someone else to hang around with. They may worry that there will be no one to sit by in the class or on the trip. They may feel pessimistic.

Children who have remained optimistic while they have been ill, might feel deflated when they go back to school and find that everyone has moved on and although they are welcomed back they will have to make some effort to re-establish themselves.

Some children who were optimistic while they were ill might feel betrayed when they get back and find that they are no longer the star that they were while they were ill. They are now just one of the crowd and they have to find a different way to fit in.

Children who were pessimistic while they were ill may find that returning to their lives now they are better is a lot easier than they thought it was going to be. People do remember them. They are offered some help and it doesn't take them very long to feel they can cope.

Other children who have been pessimistic may go in with such a negative view of what is going to happen that they make it very difficult for themselves to accept help or for people to want to give help.

Rebalancing optimism

A good way of helping children who have to rejoin something which has been going on in their absence is to arrange for them to meet up with one or two of the other children who have been going to the activity while they have been off. This meeting will give the child who has been ill and has now recovered a gentle introduction to the world he has been absent from. It will also help him feel as if he has an ally. There will be someone in the group that definitely remembers who he is.

It can be a frightening prospect to face a large group of people when you are not sure whether they will even remember your name, let alone why they used to like you. Make sure you have let the leader, organiser or teacher know that the child is coming back, and give them some idea of what the child can manage. If the child isn't going to be able to run around, or if he will need to go to the toilet more often, make sure that the person in charge knows. Otherwise the adult responsible can feel confused and uncertain and find it easier to ignore the child or limit the child in order not to put him under too much pressure.

I've got lots of places to be

Imagination is a powerful tool for building confidence. Children with imagination can see possibilities where others see nothing. Their imaginations might work overtime, and it might be quite difficult to get them to join in with something that is outside their imaginary world, but without any imagination at all they would be missing a great strength. Some children who have very powerful imaginations use their thoughts as a refuge when they are sick. They find a way to escape the difficulties of their illness and conjure up fantastical situations that keep them entertained and help them put colour into what could be a very boring or difficult time.

Imaginative children may have trouble focusing on what they are supposed to be doing, but they should be able to grasp enough of what is going on to do what is needed. They might need to be reminded of the real world and given ideas about when and where it is okay for them to enjoy their flights of fancy.

Children who don't use their imagination may find that they rely on films, videos and magazines for stimulation. When they return to school they might find that they can't generate any ideas for themselves. Before they were ill they would spark off their friends or teachers or the activities they were doing. Because they haven't been exercising their imagination while they have been ill, when they return to their lives after the illness they can't invent ways of coping with finding their place again and grasping what is going on.

Reinventing imagination

Teach children ways to relax and visualise and you will show them how to use their imagination to make their lives easier. They can imagine themselves getting on in a situation they fear and then think of ways of making that situation easier to cope with. They can hold in their mind something that gives them pleasure when they have to cope with something which they find difficult.

Teach children how to take deep breaths so that when they feel tense and trapped they can find a way of releasing the tension. Chapter 15 has a series of visualisations which will help children become motivated. Visualisation stimulates their imaginations so that they can view things from a wider angle. They will learn how to appreciate whatever they are involved in by using all their senses, their intellect and their emotions. The illness will become part of the fabric of their lives. They will be able to give it its proper place and start afresh.

Where there's a will there's a way

Willingness is probably one of the most important resources anyone, including children, can have. If children show willing then people will enjoy giving help, encouragement and time to get them started. Willing children give out an energy which means that people working with them benefit from the willing child's enthusiasm. Children who are unwilling to have a go have the opposite effect. They use up other people's precious supplies of energy and they may find themselves sidelined.

Recovering willingness

Help children to recognise who has been willing to make their lives better. Encourage them to acknowledge the willingness of others. Give children ideas of how they can show willingness themselves.

When someone has done something that helps your child, tell your child about what the person has done. Perhaps they kept an eye on the house while you were away or they found a particular book or video your child wanted and made sure they were able to have it.

Help your child write letters, make phone calls, send e-mails or postcards to people who have shown a willingness to help them. This will mean your child understands lots of ways in which people are willing to help others. People who are willing to help others are also eager to be involved in their own lives.

They see opportunities to make contributions which will add to their life as well as the lives of others. This is what you want for a child who has been ill. You want them to see how to be willing. You want them to see how they can be willing. You want them to show willing.

The girl who opted out

When Debbie had glandular fever, she couldn't go into school or keep up with any of her out-of-school activities. Her grandparents looked after her during the day while her parents were at work. They enjoyed her company and, as she got better, they started to take her out on their shopping trips. Debbie loved being with them, going to cafés and listening to them talking with their friends. As she was recovering she found she was happy to go at the pace they went at.

It was quite different at home. She couldn't cope with her sister or her sister's friends. They seemed noisy and excited all the time. They dashed around the house, changed clothes and hairstyles and then dashed around some more. Before she contracted glandular fever, Debbie had enjoyed all those things, but now she didn't want to be bothered. She lost interest in other things as well. She said she wasn't interested in going back to her drama class or to her swimming club. She was irritable with everyone at home. She did manage to go back to school. Her parents thought it would be a good idea if she was picked up by her grandparents every night rather than getting herself home. Debbie was happy with this. She would go back to her grandparents' for tea and spend a couple of hours with them watching television. When she got home, she was in a much happier frame of mind. Life settled down into a routine.

This routine was creating a dangerous situation for Debbie because she was moving into a position where she could be overlooked by everyone except her grandparents. She wasn't causing a fuss, the teachers weren't complaining about her work, her parents were busy and thought she was all right. There was really nothing new to say about Debbie. Without knowing it, Debbie had opted out. She had lost her spark.

How to help children who have been ill and who have opted out

1. Make sure they are eating healthily. They may need a vitamin supplement.
2. Find ways to help them get some gentle exercise.
3. Build up to them getting half an hour of fresh air every day.
4. Develop some optimism in them by making plans with them for the future. These can be plans for the next day or the next week. Don't be put off if children say they are not bothered or couldn't care less about any plans. Whatever you are planning, make sure there is more input than just your own. Involve other people in the family. This could be which day next week you are going to have the favourite family meal or when next week you are going to choose the colour of paint for the bathroom.
5. While it is good that children have friends of all different ages, it is important that they do have contact with children of their own age. People of the same age have so many things in common. They spark off each other because they see things in the same way. They might not agree with each other but they have special things in common which they don't have in common with anybody else. We all know that feeling.

The fundamentals of helping someone get their zest for life back:

- Don't expect immediate results
- Be inventive
- See it as a challenge
- Don't give up
- Play a long game. Kids can hold out a lot longer than you think
- Don't let it take over your life
- Try and involve other people in the child's life to help him get back his zest for living

Zest for life can be a challenge

Concentration – focusing hard on the job in hand
Happiness – openness to others who want to join in
Anticipation – looking forward to the future
Learning – trying to understand how to do something new
Loving – feeling a happy contentment at being with others with a
  zest for life too
Energy – nothing is too much trouble
Noticing – what is going on
Guts – falling off, getting up and having another go
Enchanting

With a zest for life children can take on a challenge, they can set their own challenges, and they will also accept challenges. They will be motoring. They will be motivated. They will be enchanting.

5

Helping the child who thinks he is no good

How can children end up feeling that they are no good? Children can feel no good when they:

- Have been labelled as having a problem
- Feel they have failed at something that they thought they should be able to do
- Try taking the pressure off by saying that they are no good and then end up believing that they really are no good
- Are too scared to think that they could be good
- Are compared with someone else
- See children who get ten out of ten as the only people who are any good
- Are unsure about how effort and reward are linked, and have no idea of what they could have done or could do to improve so they think they are no good
- Think that if someone finds something easy when they find it difficult this is proof that they are no good
- Give up and don't allow themselves a chance to practise, which means they can't get better

Am I any good?

Some children become anxious because they believe that they are no good. They might worry that people aren't going to be proud of them, they are taking too long to learn something, or they find what they have to do harder than everybody else.

Children need to be reassured that having a go is good, making progress is good, and moving one step forward and two steps back is normal.

Children need to be reassured that just because they can't do something well it doesn't mean they have to give it up.

Children need to be reassured that when they make a mistake there are adults and children who want to help them learn how to do it better.

You can spot a child who is anxious about whether he is any good if you know what to look for:

- Nail biting
- Hair sucking
- Fidgeting
- Hiding
- Silence
- Mumbling
- Crying
- Tension
- Frightened looks
- Clinging
- Defiance
- Feeling sick

'Mummy, I've got a tummy ache'

Ronan said he had a tummy ache and didn't want to go to school. He was very upset and didn't want to leave the house. His parents weren't sure what to do. His father thought Ronan was genuinely unwell. His mother thought he was trying to avoid school. She asked Ronan if anything was bothering him but he cried and insisted that his tummy really hurt.

Ronan's mum was not convinced. She still felt that Ronan wasn't poorly. She felt that there was probably something happening at school which he was anxious about. She decided that if her son couldn't tell his parents what it was, the best thing they could do would be to get him to school where he could explain to his teacher what the problem was. Ronan's father reluctantly agreed that Ronan should go to school but had severe misgivings when they handed a sobbing boy over to his teacher.

As they went back to the car the tension between the parents was awful. Ronan had looked so pale and so upset that even his mum was a bit worried, but she still felt sure that Ronan would be all right. She knew that if he was really ill, the teacher would ring her and she could come and pick him up. She felt that, as parents, they had to get him in to school and give the teacher the opportunity to solve the problem. It was a chance she had to take.

As the two parents reached the car in silence, Ronan's teacher came running after them with the news that Ronan was already happily playing. When a child had asked Ronan if he wanted to play football, Ronan had immediately taken up the invitation. He had skipped off to join the game. There was no sign of illness. The teacher said that she would try to have a chat with Ronan at some point in the day to find out what he had been worried about.

When Ronan's dad picked him up after school, Ronan ran out happily. He couldn't even remember that he had had a tummy ache.

Sometimes someone else has the answer

It can be nerve-wracking for parents when they have to judge which way they need to respond in this sort of situation. Should they give support or should they give in?

Ronan's parents took the chance and decided that school was probably the best place for Ronan to get help with whatever was bothering him. They were lucky that Ronan rushed off to join his friends so quickly. They were fortunate, too, that Ronan's teacher knew that parents need reassurance that they are doing the right thing and came out to tell them that Ronan's anxiety appeared to have gone.

Parents need reassurance that other adults can have goodwill towards their children and want to help them move forward. They need reassurance that even good parents will meet problems sometimes. They need reassurance that other adults have goodwill towards them and want to help them in any way they can. Finally, parents need reassurance that other parents are finding it just as tricky to bring up their children.

Letting children free themselves from anxiety

If Ronan had been anxious about something specific in school, his parents had given him the chance to discover that often what you are worried about doesn't happen. Once you get going, you often see the difficulty in a different way. Sometimes it has disappeared. Sometimes it still needs to be sorted out. Ronan could have been worried that the work was going to be too hard, that he wouldn't have a friend to play with, or that someone was going to find out that it was he who had broken something yesterday. Things can go wrong for all of us. All of us can become anxious about things that are going to happen and how they may go wrong. All of us need the chance to know that worrying is a waste of time because 'it might never happen'.

Ronan got the chance to see that just because one thing had gone wrong, or he was worried about something that might go wrong, he did not have to run away from his life completely.

Stopping worries taking over

Children see things in black and white. They can be taken over by whatever they have given their attention to. Many children become completely absorbed in their coming birthday, holiday or trip to the funfair. It could still be three weeks away but the child thinks of nothing else and talks of nothing else and expects everyone else to think and talk about nothing else as well. When children have a worry, they can be absorbed by it in just the same way but usually for a shorter time. They think of nothing else.

If one person is horrible at school, they can't think of all the other people that like them. That is why children will often gravitate to the child that is giving them a problem. They just can't see all the other possibilities that wouldn't cause them grief.

If one topic is difficult to understand, they feel that school is too hard or they will have to give up that subject at the earliest possible opportunity. They can't see what they have already managed to learn so far and trust that they will get the hang of this tricky topic if they keep at it. They need help to redirect their attention away from hating the topic towards working out how to tackle it.

Fear of falling further

If a child has been dropped an ability group, they can feel that they must never have been any good. They worry that the only moves they are going to make in the future will be down. They become so worried about their reversal in fortune that they stop working and just worry. From this position it is very likely that they will be moved down again. They need help to put the fear of repeated failure to one side and to get on with the work they are being given so that they can use this setback positively. Now they know how much work they have to do if they want to be successful.

It takes time and patience to help children know that they can still be liked, loved and respected even if they think they are not perfect. Because children see the world in black and white, they will try and lead you to tell them that they are absolutely dreadful or that the teacher is no good because the teacher doesn't think that they are great. This is your opportunity to help your children understand that when they have done something that isn't up to the required standard, any judgement made about their work isn't personal. Children who think they are no good can use a poor mark, or a mark they think is poor, as a stick to beat themselves (or anybody else) with.

The wider view

If you can teach your children how to take a wider view then their awareness will develop. Not all children are born with an understanding that there are many different ways of approaching a problem. Children who don't know that there are will become anxious, feel they are not liked or that they are no good.

I know I'm no good

Clare was poor at maths but very good at English. She wanted to do well in school and was worried that her maths would let her down. She tried really hard but she just couldn't seem to progress in maths in the same way that she could in English. She decided she was hopeless at maths and this was never going to change. She became withdrawn. She hunched her shoulders up to her ears. She looked out of frightened eyes. She was pale. She was reluctant to give an answer to anything to do with maths. If she thought that a question was going to be about maths, she would be defensive – even if the question was nothing to do with maths and was actually about something she had done at the weekend. It was very difficult to teach Clare any maths because her defences were up so high that the energy level needed from anyone trying to help her was enormous.

It can be exhausting helping children who think they are no good as they spend all their time and energy trying to convince whoever is helping them to give up on them. They want everyone to feel, like they do, that they will never be able to do it.

Anxious children who need huge amounts of energy from people trying to help them usually end up missing out. They miss out because however good are the intentions of the teacher, parent or carer there is a limit to how much energy they can put into helping the children in any given session.

Children who are very anxious can have a negative effect on anybody who is trying to help them. Whatever is suggested is ignored, argued about or seen as impossible. Somebody in the grip of anxiety can have difficulty hearing suggestions which will help them overcome the problem and therefore the anxiety.

Staying sane

If you are trying to help a child who is determined to convince you that he can't do it, you really need to have something else to occupy a part of your mind. Otherwise you will find yourself sucked in to his negativity. You will start to feel despondent and begin to doubt that you can help this child. You will become depressed at the idea of having to do anything with the child.

Helpful strategies for staying sane

1. Have another child working alongside:
   - The working relationship you build with the second child can act as a good model for the anxious child
   - Instead of it being a battle of wills between one person who is determined something will happen and another person who is equally determined that nothing will happen, it becomes a positive experience as you work with the other child
   - The negative child often starts to become involved in spite of himself
   - Children are great supporters of each other in situations like this. They can often find words which will make more sense to the child who is negative when you can't think of anything positive to say
   - The other child can be working on the same activity or a different activity
   - Your mind will have an opportunity to have a break from the deadening effect of a one-way conversation

2. If you are only working with one child, have a crossword or a word-search you can do when the child is trying something on their own:
   - Choose something that will not distract you completely but will give your brain a chance to work on finding a solution

- You will be giving an example of how to focus, how to persist and how to think about something
- You will be giving an example of stillness, quietness and calmness which will help to diffuse some of the anxiety

3. Have a book handy which you can read when the child is working:
   - You will be offering companionship
   - You will be demonstrating absorption
   - You will be showing that you can be deeply interested in something that is written down
   - It will take the pressure off

By following these suggestions you won't be worn down by the child's agitation and anxiety. You will get energy back into what you are doing with the child. Instead of feeling that you are losing control, you will be able to maintain control over your own behaviour even if you can't make progress with the anxious child that time.

If you have lost your temper, become agitated or irritated, that is what the child will remember when you try to work together again. Using the strategies above will help you avoid stress but if you do get cross or cranky with the child don't waste energy worrying about it, work out what support you will need for the next time.

If you have remained even-tempered, calm and confident, the child will recall that atmosphere when they sit down with you the next time. You will be able to reassure the child that even if the problem hasn't gone away yet, if you both keep trying you will be able to sort it out this time.

Sometimes children can look so anxious that they appear to have a real learning difficulty. They look so bewildered and vulnerable that you feel you shouldn't be trying to teach them anything.

I know she's no Einstein but . . .

Sophie was nine but her reading and spelling age were way below that level. She had got stuck on the bottom rung of the ladder and she seemed incapable of going any further. All of her teachers would offer her the choice of whether she did an activity or not.

When she was doing maths, she could choose whether she would colour in or whether she would try to do something a little more difficult. Always her choices were to do the simplest tasks.

When the class was going to perform for the rest of the school, she was allowed to decide whether she wanted to take part or not.

Some of the teachers at Sophie's school felt that Sophie's problem was a matter of confidence but they couldn't find a way to motivate Sophie and get her to realise that the level she was operating at was really not the level where she needed to be. They felt that Sophie should be able to do more but they didn't know how to help her break through the barrier they felt was there.

A classroom assistant was arranged but still Sophie failed to make progress. Her parents were anxious. They felt that they had an intelligent child because in some situations, at dancing class or at Sunday School, Sophie would be equal to other children of her age group.

Eventually Sophie was judged to be in need of a place at a special school. She was horrified because she didn't want to leave her friends. Her teacher explained to her parents that Sophie would have to speak to teachers and do the work at least to a level where she could be taught in the class if she wanted to stay at the school. The teachers had to feel that she could make progress and that she was in the right place for her educational needs.

When Sophie understood that she wouldn't be offered choices again and that she would be expected simply to do the work that other children in her group were being set, she got on with it. She hadn't understood that the choices she was making previously should not have been made. She had thought that because she was no good she really had to choose the easy option every time. She had not realised that the teachers were giving her harder options as well because they felt that with help and teaching Sophie would be able to do those tasks.

What is a teacher?

Some children don't understand the role of a teacher. Children think if the teacher has given them some work they should be able to do it. Children don't realise that teachers are expecting them to ask questions if they are stuck.

Children also don't realise that teachers will expect them to make mistakes. They don't understand what a teacher does with a mistake. Children don't understand that if you get a cross on your work it doesn't mean that the teacher is cross.

If you have a child who thinks he is no good, it is quite likely that he has misunderstood what he needs to do when he is trying to learn something.

You can help children like this by explaining how hard it is for anyone to learn something new. You can refer to something that someone in the family is learning. You can explain what you do when you need to learn something new at work, at home or when you are out with your friends.

They need to know:

1. Why teachers give pupils work:
   - To check how much of what they have taught has been understood
   - To check how much of what they have taught has been remembered
   - To see how much pupils already know
   - To see how pupils work on their own
   - To see how pupils work as a group
   - To see how much pupils can get done in a set time
   - To keep pupils busy
   - To see what needs to be taught next

and what they do with the information they gather:

- Decide what to teach next
- Work out who needs what help
- Decide what needs to be practised
- Decide what they need to say to the parents
- Build up a picture of each pupil as well as the class as a whole
- Decide who would work well together

2. Why teachers put children into groups:
   - So the children can work together and help each other
   - So children can work at the same pace
   - So that everything doesn't have to be explained to the whole class or to individuals
   - To share equipment
   - To make it easier to teach a smaller group something new while other children get on with something else

3. Why teachers put marks and comments on work:
   - To show that they have looked at the work
   - To give pupils an idea of how well they have done
   - To give pupils an idea of what they can do to make it better next time
   - To remind the pupil to ask them about the work
   - To provide an audience for the work that has been done
   - So somebody else can check up that the teacher has seen everybody's work

The A–Z of a good teaching experience
Children will gain:

Ambition
Belief in themselves
Confidence
Dignity
Enthusiasm
Frameworks
Guidance

Help
Inspiration
Justice
Knowledge
Leadership
Motivation
Notes
Optimism
Power
Quality control
Respect
Skills
Tuition
Understanding
Values
Warnings
eXcitement
Yearnings
Zeal

The A–Z of a bad teaching experience
Children will become:

Anxious
Bored
Complacent
Demotivated
Exhausted
Fraught
Grouchy
Helpless
Intimidated
Jaded
Knocked
Lethargic
Miserable

Neglected
Obstinate
Pessimistic
Quarrelsome
Restless
Sidelined
Thoughtless
Unskilled
Vague
Weak
eXploited
Yawning
Zapped

How to turn a bad teaching experience round

The first thing to remember is that teachers will welcome the opportunity to teach well. When a teaching situation goes wrong a pupil can help to get it right. Body language plays a large part in the quality of the experience. If children slouch, yawn, fidget or fiddle, teachers can have difficulty keeping their focus. If children sit up straight, look as if they are alert and look as if they are ready to do what is being asked, teachers find it very easy to keep their focus, their train of thought and their awareness of what their pupils need next.

Children need to know that teachers need positive feedback in the same way that pupils do. Teachers need children to be looking at them when they are speaking, answering or listening to the answers to questions when there is a question-and-answer session, and they need them to behave as supportive members of the group. Children are very easily led and one or two children who decide to work with the teacher to make the experience productive or positive can be as powerful as one or two children who decide to work against the teacher.

One of the reasons teachers give for leaving the profession is the futility they feel when faced with a class who are unwilling to learn. For many years unruly classes were seen to be the fault of the teacher. Teachers were trained to be more entertaining, to be friends with their pupils and to make learning 'fun'. Pupils grew to expect learning to be made easy. They expected to get good marks for any work that was handed in. They expected to be able to blame the teacher if they found something difficult. Children need to understand that teaching and learning is a two-way process. Good teachers make good learners and good learners can make good teachers.

Sometimes motivated children will be in unruly classes. At times they will have teachers who are unprepared. They will have teachers who are preoccupied with problems in their personal lives or with their duties within the school.

Motivated children can be helped to survive in these circumstances. They need to see the situation from the teacher's point of view. They need to have alternatives for when the teacher is unable to give them direct teaching or help when they are stuck. They need to know that their education is dependent on the effort they put in. Teachers can enhance that effort. Everyone, even children, is responsible for his own effort and for developing independent learning skills.

6

Helping the child who thinks it doesn't matter

Why do children think that important things which they are expected to do, or are asked to do, don't matter?

- They have been given poor models for how to respond
- They have been given choices about their own responsibilities too early
- There has been conflict about what should or shouldn't matter
- They haven't understood consequences
- They have picked up the idea that the rules don't apply to them
- They have deliberately ignored something
- They are ignorant about the role they should play and how they are supposed to play it
- They expect rewards, encouragement and reminders before they will even consider having a go, as previously they have been rewarded and bribed when there really was no need

Big gaps for Tom

Tom had been at a different school and in a different education system because he had been abroad for two years. His parents

71

had been working overseas and he had attended the local school near where they had been renting an apartment. Tom had started off at school in England. He had done two years in primary school before his two years abroad. He had enjoyed both settings. He had settled in well and while abroad had got to grips with languages in the way that young children can. Tom looked forward to getting back to school in England because he wanted to learn how to play cricket, which wasn't taught in the school abroad.

Before he started the school in England he went along with his mum and dad for a chat with his new head teacher. While he was there he was asked to do a few worksheets so that his new teacher would have an idea of where he was up to. It hadn't crossed Tom's mind that he might not be at the same place as all the other children. It also hadn't crossed his mind that there might be a new teacher and a new head teacher. He looked a little worried at the idea of having to do some work in front of the head teacher but she told him that it didn't matter what he put, she only wanted to know what he could do.

Once Tom was at school he didn't find things too bad. The teacher knew that he hadn't learned a lot of the things that the rest of her class had and she gave him easier work while he caught up. Tom could do the easy work and was quite happy. The teacher seemed happy and told his mum that he was settling in well. She said she was giving him time to find his feet before she got on with the serious business. She had no worries that Tom would be able to learn what she had to teach him but she had to wait until she had the time spare to be able to introduce him to the things he would need to know. When Tom's mother offered to do the work at home the teacher said she would prefer to do it with Tom at school because she would be able to link it in with other things they were doing in class.

The best laid plans

Tom enjoyed the special place he had in the class. He was popular. Other children were very interested when he told them about his time abroad. Occasionally he would say something for them in one of the languages he had picked up. All in all, being back in England was going very well for Tom.

However, inadvertently, the message that Tom had picked up was that he did not have to do what everyone else was doing and it didn't matter that he wasn't doing the same as everybody else. He was happy about that. He enjoyed being different.

Tom felt he was different and that difference had to be preserved. He kept on looking for something that would reveal how different he was.

There were times when Tom could have done the work that the rest of the class was doing but the teacher hadn't realised and so he carried on with what he had been given.

After a while, Tom's teacher tried to start giving extra help to Tom and sometimes asked him to do the same work as everyone else. He would always find a reason why he couldn't manage to do what he had been asked:

- If everyone was looking up the dictionary to find the same word, Tom would insist that he had searched the dictionary but the word wasn't in his copy
- When a parent or a helper worked with him, he would report that they hadn't told him what everyone else had been told or that they had distracted him
- When everyone had heard an explanation of the work they were to do or the activity they were to move on to, Tom would say that he wasn't quite sure what was happening. He liked to say that he was quite confused about what he was supposed to do

Tom went from being popular for himself to being unpopular because he was always saying he had a problem and often held up activities while his 'problem' was sorted out.

Tom no longer felt himself to be an equal in any situation. He was caught in a trap but didn't realise it. He thought that rules and requests applied to everyone else but not to him. He was never embarrassed about the reasons why he couldn't do things. He believed them all to be true. He didn't know that what he thought was wrong.

Tom's excuses

Things 'disappeared'. Someone had taken his ruler, he had put his pen down on the table and now it wasn't there, when he went out to check in his bag he couldn't find the note his mum had given him, although everyone else had found paper he couldn't find any. Things didn't work. His pencil was broken, the computer he was working on was slower than everyone else's, his pen kept leaking, the pencil sharpener he had been given was too small for the pencil he had to sharpen.

It went on and on. There was always a kerfuffle around Tom. Tom tried to involve as many people as possible.

If he couldn't think of any other way of showing how he was different, he would say that he hadn't heard, he didn't understand or that he was still quite confused.

Tom wasn't bothered when people got irritated. He didn't seem to notice. He was always busy concentrating on the things that made him different from everyone else. He didn't think it mattered that although everyone else gave in a completed work-sheet his had barely been started. Tom didn't think it mattered that other children finished their homework and gave it in and that he didn't. He didn't think it mattered that he wasn't getting through the reading books and the maths books as fast as everybody else.

When the best intentions of teachers and parents go wrong

Tom's mum and teacher had thought that it was reasonable to give Tom a chance to settle down. They knew that it was only a temporary situation and that soon Tom would catch up with most of the work. They hadn't bargained on how Tom would interpret what was happening.

For Tom there was a genuine situation, coming back after a two-year break, which meant that there was a real reason for him to need special consideration. Although the adults knew the situation was temporary, Tom didn't. Tom had constructed an attitude to school based on his understanding. He understood that because he had come back after two years he would be treated differently. He didn't understand that he would be expected to be the same as everybody else pretty quickly, even if he needed some extra help in some subjects.

Tom had decided that his personal situation should always be considered. There would always be a reason why he couldn't do what he had been asked to do. He looked for reasons why he couldn't get on and do something. He expected to find reasons why it would be impossible for him to get on.

Look for the solution – don't look for excuses

The challenge for people who care for children is in helping children to see how they can overcome a difficulty. Tom wasn't involved in the discussion about how he could catch up. He was unintentionally sidelined. He constructed his own idea about what was happening and the way he was to handle it. Even when he overheard lessons that he could have taken part in, he didn't suggest that he join in because he had identified himself as someone for whom it didn't matter that he wasn't joining in.

Tom did what he did because that was what he thought was expected. He had never tried to avoid work before and had never been difficult in class. He had genuinely thought the adults were saying that it didn't matter if he didn't do the work everyone else was doing.

Other children might have heard exactly the same conversations as Tom yet have reacted in a totally different way. Other children might not have expected to continue being different from the rest of the group. Other children might not have expected to be unable to do something, and other children might have avoided work in other ways, based on the way they had made sense of what was going on.

What Tom needed to know

Tom needed to know that he had been allowed to develop a habit without anybody realising it. This habit had to be let go. In future, he would be expected to do what other people were doing. He would have to finish his work, hand his homework in on time, know where his equipment was, and generally be like everyone else. He would be helped to overcome his habit. If he couldn't find something when other children could, such as the paper, he would need to spend some of his break making sure he knew where things were kept in the classroom. If he couldn't understand what had been explained, he wasn't to interrupt. He was to write down all the things he needed to know. He was to write down the reasons he felt he couldn't do the work and the questions he would need to ask to have the information that would mean he could do the work. Once he had finished writing down all the reasons he could think of he could carry on with the easier work that he had been doing while he settled into the class and the school.

What Tom's parents were able to do

Tom's parents had no idea that he was falling behind in school. The teacher had said she would ensure he filled in the gaps in his learning and had asked the parents to leave it to her. At home, Tom was his normal self, willing to pit himself against a whole variety of challenges, and growing up in a way that brought pleasure to his parents. They were surprised when the school said how badly he was doing and met with the teacher to find out what was going on. Meeting the teacher and then talking to Tom they realised what had happened. They also realised how important it was that they support the teacher in the steps she was making to help Tom become someone who realised that what he did mattered.

A home-/school-book was started that Tom took into school each morning and brought home each evening. In the book his teacher would note down what he had finished and what work was still outstanding. His parents would make sure that he had finished any outstanding work and write a note to the teacher to let her know how it had gone.

If Tom maintained that he really didn't know what he was supposed to do, then his parents would set him some other work which he would take into school and put a note in the book explaining what they had done and why. This then gave the teacher the chance to see what Tom was showing he could do and what he was saying he couldn't do. It allowed for follow up. If Tom told his parents that he couldn't do a piece of work, his parents would write a note to the teacher and the teacher would make sure she gave him some help or set him some work, which would mean he could learn what it was that he felt he didn't know.

This level of support for Tom's progress meant that the problem was sorted out very quickly.

It did not take Tom long to realise that he could do more than he had been doing and that people were expecting him to do more.

Tom began to see that saying he couldn't do something did not mean he should stop.

He also started to realise that whatever people said to him he could set his own high standard.

Many children will have times when they are different to everyone else. They can choose to make these differences into difficulties and insist on distancing themselves from their peer group. Alternatively, they can acknowledge that there is a difference but not use the difference as a way of getting out of things they could do.

It is important for parents to help children find ways in which they can be included, use their capacities to the full and develop their potential.

When a child isn't motivated to sort out the details because they think someone else will do it for them

Joel's parents were pleased to help him get the most out of his life. Joel felt this meant that getting the most out of his life was the only part he had to play. He would perform and his parents would be his chauffeur, his secretary and his financier. If he was playing for the local youth team in a football match after school, he wouldn't bother to find out where it was or what time he needed to be there, he would just expect one of his parents to be sitting in the car outside the school with two bags on the back seat. One bag would have his football strip in it and the other would have sandwiches and drinks. There would always be plenty of sandwiches because in the course of the day Joel would probably have offered a lift to someone else on the team. Whichever parent was driving would know where to go because they would have found out where the match was being held and how to get there. Both parents had busy jobs and it was hard for them to arrange getting Joel to all the places he needed to be but they just about managed. Then Joel announced that he had volunteered to paint the scenery for the school play for the next three Sunday mornings. That was the last straw. Joel knew that his parents really enjoyed their rest on a Sunday morning. It had always been precious family time when the pressures were off and the car could stay in the driveway.

What matters to me is important: what matters to other people doesn't matter to me at all

Joel thought his activities were the most important thing that his family had to consider. His parents had thought this too. But when it looked like they were going to lose some of their Sunday mornings they reconsidered their priorities. Sunday mornings really mattered to them. It was their chance to recharge their batteries, relax and recuperate together. Up until now, they had done this together as a family. Joel could be part of Sunday morning but he could not ruin Sunday morning even if he wanted to do something else. He could not feel that his parents' Sunday mornings did not matter.

Joel's parents decided not to have a row about it. They explained to Joel that this was something he could work out for himself. He could organise his own lift or catch the bus.

Joel was surprised, but then he was happy to accept the challenge. He found out who else was going and that they were getting there by bus. He met his friends at the bus stop and they all went together.

It didn't take long for Joel to sort himself out over Sunday mornings and, having been given the chance to grow up in this way, he also began to sort out other things for himself.

It is important that children realise that when people do things for them it does matter. Your children will have no motivation to learn how to be independent if you always do everything for them. They need to know what they have to do in order to organise how to get somewhere when they need to. They need to have a go at doing it so they realise how many pitfalls there are when you try and organise anything. They need to have the chances to deal with those pitfalls so they will still be motivated to take on new experiences for themselves.

If you have got into the same position as Joel's parents
- You have to want to change
- You have to know why you want to change
- You have to know it is reasonable for you to want to change because you want some of your own life back
- You have to know it is reasonable that children begin to find ways of being able to do the things they want to do

What matters to other people doesn't matter in our family

Some families pride themselves on doing things differently from everybody else. They have thought about the conventions and decided that they are not for them. They tend to choose friends who feel the same way. As their children get older and want to have friends that aren't family friends, they can hit a difficulty. Families have different standards about all sorts of things, including tidying up, politeness, swearing and taking care of other people's property.

My mum and dad don't think it matters

It can be difficult for children if their parents only teach a single standard. If they only have one standard, children will believe absolutely that the way they have been allowed to behave or taught to behave is right in every situation. They become a problem wherever this is not the case. Other people are not motivated to invite them round or take them out on trips because they don't want the stress of worrying about having to check up on the child all the time.

She's your friend

Steven had met Amy at the youth club. He was fascinated by her and when she said she liked going for walks as well, he asked his family if she could come with them the next time.

From the moment they picked Amy up things felt awkward. Amy kept making remarks in a loud voice about other people. She and Steven would run on ahead and when Steven's parents called them back, they would run on even further so that they were out of earshot.

Steven's parents were horrified when they saw Amy and Steven wrestling in the middle of the path forcing other people who were out for a walk to skirt round them. The children seemed to have no idea of the impression they were creating. Steven's parents couldn't believe what they were seeing. By the time they caught up with Amy and Steven, Amy was swinging on a tree and as they got to her the branch snapped. Amy giggled hysterically while Steven snorted. He knew his parents were not pleased and his embarrassment and shock made him laugh.

The only thing Steven's parents felt they could do was to turn round and take the children home. When they got home they said to Amy that if she wanted to come for a walk with them again they would need to talk about where they were going and how they would expect herself and Steven to behave.

They explained to Steven that it mattered to them how people behaved when they were out on a walk and they didn't want to take Amy if she was going to spoil the walk for them and for other people as well.

Amy was intrigued by what Steven's parents and Steven had told her and was motivated to learn another way of behaving that was different from the one she had learned with her parents.

Children who have been brought up to know that different situations and different sets of people demand different ways of behaving are more likely to be offered experiences that will give them more choices in their lives.

If parents see themselves as only wacky or caring or highly motivated or laid back, then they may be unable to teach their children that there are times when you can be different.

Most families have a strong sense of the sort of people they are and there is nothing wrong with this. They have different standards for different situations. Children learn in these families that sometimes their parents behave in one way or allow them to behave in one way. At other times they are expected to behave in a different way. They might slump in front of the television with their feet on the coffee-table in their own home, but won't do that when they go to visit or when they have visitors. They might have furniture they can climb on at home but they must never climb on furniture in someone else's house.

Children who understand appropriate behaviour learn to look for signals that will help them know how to behave. They are motivated to find out how they can fit in. They are motivated to fit in without losing their own identity and sense of right and wrong. They are motivated to expand their world. They are open to new experiences. They also have a strong sense of the code they have been taught. Gradually, they find ways to incorporate what they think is worthwhile, that they have picked up from other situations, into their own lives.

The source of lots of our motivation as adults is what we were influenced by as children.

All through your life you are striking a balance between what you know, what you need to protect yourself, what you are motivated to do next and how you can take steps to achieve your goal.

7

Helping the child who doesn't want to grow up

What is growing up?

Growing up is about learning to take responsibility for keeping things safe. The things that need to be kept safe are people, belongings, time, energy and self-esteem. Children who haven't matured so that their behaviour is similar to others in their age group find it difficult to keep things safe. Their actions can appear silly, dangerous, selfish, wilful and mean. In the same circumstances other children will be careful, pleasant and generous or fair.

Some children don't want to grow up because:

- They are only responded to when they are acting as a baby or younger than their years
- They have not been given the skills and the tools to cope at the age they are
- They have given up trying to get people to see them as the age that they are
- They haven't been given dignity and haven't been taught how to be reasonable

Helping a baby grow up

Let's take the example of a baby and a ball. We give small children soft, light balls for them to play with. They discover the fun of dropping, rolling and tossing the ball. They are unlikely to do any harm to themselves, others or what is around them if the ball they are given is soft and light enough for them to have been able to pick it up in the first place. It is safe to let them play with the ball.

Growing up means staying safe

A small child will be supervised and lots of information will be being passed on even though the child may not have the language to understand it.

The information the child will pick up as he grows up will be where he can play with a ball and how he can play with a ball so that he is safe. As children demonstrate they understand the information they will be given balls that are bigger or heavier.

Children who don't pick up the information about how to handle playing with a ball start to become a liability as their growing strength and capacity to move means they can handle weightier balls, throw and kick them with more force and run after them with greater speed.

They are likely to cause damage if they are so focused on the fun they are having with the ball that they don't notice where they are, what others are saying, or what is likely to happen. They are not safe with a ball that would be OK for other children of their age.

The boy who could kick a ball, even if it was straight through the window

Jacob was thrilled when he learned to control a ball with his feet. For many years he had been on the sidelines whenever there was a group playing because he couldn't work out how to make the moves enabling him to intercept a ball when it was in play. When he did learn how to do this, he was determined not to let the ball out of his control. Everything he did was to make sure no one else could get the ball from him. He would run over flowerbeds, crash into people in the area, and ignore anyone who tried to get him to play more as a member of a team. Jacob was not an unpleasant boy but he was so excited at getting hold of the ball, and there was so much he felt he could do with the ball, that everything else faded away.

Four steps to successful and safe play

Coaches of football or any other game know there are stages that children go through when learning to play as a team:

1. Very young children are random.
2. Slightly older children hunt as a pack with every player chasing the ball and no idea of which direction their team should be heading in.
3. The next step is selfishness. This was where Jacob was. Many of us will recognise how easy it is for us to be selfish when we think about how we have 'helped' a younger child learn how to play with a ball. We take the child out to the garden, supposedly to teach them something new, and they have to stand in admiration on the sidelines while we show them how it should be done. Then, when it's their turn, what a surprise, it's time to go in!
4. The final stage is when a child learns how to balance the chance to play with the skills needed to make a good game. These skills for ball games are:
   • Using the other team members
   • Encouraging yourself and others
   • Being ready to react if the ball comes your way
   • Being ready to react if the ball is going the wrong way
   • Staying aware of the surroundings and taking responsibility to protect them

Mature motivation

These skills can be translated into whatever children are doing.

- Children who use resources such as people or things in order to make a situation better show motivation
- Children who encourage themselves and others create a motivating atmosphere
- Children who are ready to respond when things go as they hoped help keep motivation high
- Children who will stay involved even when things are unpredictable or difficult give everyone space to regroup
- Children who care about where they are and with whom they are motivate others to join in. Those other children know it is worth joining in and they know they will feel safe

Knowing how to play fair is a skill

This skill matters because when children are in the playground, the classroom, at home or out in public, everyone will feel more relaxed if everybody can trust each other.

When children don't have this skill and start behaving badly or acting irresponsibly, it is very difficult to give them opportunities which will naturally increase their motivation. They may get stuck and lose their motivation to grow up.

Richard was motivated to grow up

Richard had saved up to get a large stunt kite and he wanted to take it to the beach and play with it with his younger cousins. His dad suggested that Richard should make sure he could handle the kite before he took on looking after younger children as well. Richard saw the sense in this suggestion and practised on his own until he felt quite able to handle the kite and what it might do. Then he offered to take his two cousins with him to the beach so they could play with it together. The delight of his cousins and the pride of his parents spurred Richard on to learn even more stunts, not only for his own pleasure but because he enjoyed the fun others got from watching what he could do and then trying to do what he had taught them.

Lewis was shown how to grow up

Lewis wanted to go out with his mates to skateboard in the supermarket car park when it was empty. His parents agreed and gave him a time when he had to be home. Lewis got home late and said that he had been having so much fun he had forgotten to look at his watch. His parents then wouldn't let him go out with his friends for a week and explained that getting himself home at the right time was part of being good at skateboarding.

It is important that children learn to see the bigger picture and that caring about time is as important as caring about people or equipment.

Act your age and see what happens

Melissa was twelve. She was completely egocentric. She could not see anything from anybody else's point of view. At home she would flounce, pout and sulk. She would shout, slam doors and swear. She felt she was big enough and old enough to have some independence and do what she wanted.

Melissa at school was very immature. She hadn't grasped how to behave so the teachers could rely on her to get on with her work, hand her homework in and have friends. She was always 'on report' and felt aggrieved that the teachers never got off her back. She felt she was being treated like a child.

Melissa had never learned how to be involved in anything. She just tried to make sure that she never had to do anything she didn't want to do and got her own way when it was something she did want to do. She had never learned how to be involved with other people so she had no idea that growing up was give and take. Because she would only ever take, other people didn't see her as growing up.

Why involvement matters

The sad penalty for people who don't learn how to be involved is a limitation on life. They will not be included in many activities with other people because they are not good company.

They will find it difficult to have hobbies because hobbies require involvement, and they will find it difficult to have friends because friends require involvement.

Melissa had no understanding that her parents would be able to agree to many of her requests if she showed that she was motivated to become involved at a sensible level in her own life.

What is involvement?

Involvement can be sitting very still

Sitting still is an underrated activity. Children can often think that nothing is happening if someone is still. They can feel they don't exist if they are being still. Some children are never still enough to find out what is really happening, so they either try to set the agenda themselves so that what is going on is what they have started, or they constantly try and take over what is going on so that they feel involved.

You can free your children from this state of wanting to control everything by teaching them how to become a good observer.

You can help your children understand that when they join a group there are ways of finding out what has been going on by just watching. They can look out for:

- Who is speaking
- What they are speaking about
- Who is doing something
- Where people are sitting or standing
- How people are sitting or standing

Involvement can be eye contact

A lot of children don't ever feel involved because they don't make eye contact. Help children understand that looking at a person when you are speaking to them will make them feel involved with you. Looking at the person who is speaking to you will help you feel involved with them. When you are in a group and one person is speaking, you must check whether you need to be listening. If you should be listening, make sure you pay attention to the person who is speaking. If you don't need to be listening, then pay attention to what you should be doing.

Involvement can be the direction of your gaze

Teach children that they don't always have to make eye contact to show that they are involved in a group. Looking in the direction of what is being talked about shows people that they are involved. Gazing out of the window when everyone else is looking at something in the room will cut them off from the others. Relationships are two-way things and people can only relate when they feel that they matter and what they are doing matters as well.

Involvement can be listening out for clues

It is important that every person develops the art of keeping some part of their mind free to be able to pick up clues that will tell them what has happened, is happening or will happen next. Without this, motivation collapses because there is no involvement in or information about the activity they are supposed to be doing. Clues don't invite children to do something; they build up their knowledge about what is going on.

As children get good at listening out for clues they move on to being able to hear cues. Cues invite them to do something.

Involvement can be spotting where you can be of help, recognising that you can give help, and recognising that you can receive help

Help is anything that progresses the activity. It is helpful when children notice that someone else has joined the group and needs space. It is helpful when children try and assess what help is needed. Not all help is helpful if it cuts across the aims of the group.

Involvement can be noticing when you have or know something that could be useful

Teach children that it is important to be sensitive to the needs of the activity and of the people involved in the activity. It shows that they recognise that the person organising the activity needs their help.

Involvement can be working out the pace

Explain that if they don't work out the pace then other people will have to be responsible for adjusting so that they can fit in. This could slow down the activity or lead to it being abandoned altogether. If they don't work out the pace they could be left out. They can work out the pace by listening for cues and clues, watching other people, and being ready to come in when it is their turn.

Involvement can be recognising that you have a responsibility

Whether children decide to be passive or active in a group, their contribution will have an effect. If they look apathetic, they take energy from the group. If they are quiet and interested, they add energy to the group. If they are active but have the pace wrong they will take energy from the group. If they are taking an active part and they have got the pace right they will add energy to the group.

Involvement can mean loyalty

Sometimes children have to be loyal to themselves. They have to know the sort of person that they are and make sure this is reflected in what they do. If they are in a disruptive group, they can stay loyal to their principles. If they are in a supportive group, they can stay loyal to the aims of the group. If they are in a supportive group with some disruptive members they need to stay loyal to their principles and to the aims of the group.

Involvement can mean sharing

Because human beings are social creatures it is natural to share. Children who know how to share have a greater scope for development as they create an energy that means people are happy to involve them or be involved with them. The whole thing starts to snowball because there is no reason for the motivation to stop.

Involvement can mean caring

Children who are involved care about the quality of what is happening. They understand that quality matters. They do the best they can naturally because they enjoy feeling positive about what they are involved in. They create energy in other people to get enthusiastic about what they have done. Enthusiasm plus quality is a powerful mixture for increasing and sustaining motivation.

Involvement can be recognising the needs of others

If children don't recognise the needs of others they will become demotivated because the amount of energy that they need to put in to make sure that what they want to happen happens might make them think that it is not worth it. If they recognise the needs of others then they will be able to adjust to those needs and find some way of coping with those needs in the activity.

Involvement can be listening to what is being said

Many children get into a habit of thinking that the only time they need to listen is when someone is talking directly to them. Children who do this don't become involved because they simply don't notice what is going on. They can feel surprised or left out when suddenly the rest of the group gets up or starts on a new activity which they had no idea was about to happen. The reason they didn't know that it was about to happen was because the conversation or the instructions were general and not aimed at them in particular.

A child who ignores anything that is not directed especially at them can feel rejected or unimportant. They haven't learned that they are not the centre of everybody's universe. They haven't learned that sometimes they are an individual on their own and then their needs matter the most. At other times they are a part of a group and their own needs are not as important as the needs of the whole group. A child like this can become a liability to have in a group. They can think that wanting to stop and look at something when everyone else moves on, or wandering off in a different direction to everyone else, is quite reasonable and manageable. A child who can hear what is being said when they are in a group benefits themselves and the group. They know what is going on and so they feel confident that they can take part. Other people feel confident they can take part as well.

Involvement can be noticing what is being done

Some children live in their own heads all the time. They are fascinated by their own thoughts and their own ideas. This is fine as long as they keep an eye on what is being done. If they don't, then they become a drain on everyone else because they have to be watched out for, reminded and chased up. People are constantly having to check on them – that they are where they should be, have what they should have and have done what they should have done.

Involvement can be contributing what you can

Even babies contribute what they can. When they give a smile or a happy gurgle everybody responds and the baby feels even more involved. A child who becomes withdrawn from involvement creates indifference or tension. Many children like this become unmotivated because they think nobody is interested in them or that people don't like them. They don't realise that a smile, a helpful action or a word to show they have heard, will give people a chance to notice them, approve of them and acknowledge them.

Involvement can be accepting the chance to be a good model

Children will very quickly copy the behaviour of others. If the behaviour they copy is silly, then a situation can get out of control very quickly. Adults will then stop the whole activity or send the child who can't behave well and show a good example away from the group. The child who was silly can end up feeling that it wasn't fair because everyone else was silly as well. The child needs to learn that if you are in a group, whatever you do will be noticed. If you are behaving sensibly, the activity can continue. The child needs to understand that when something is running smoothly no comment might be made, but if someone is doing something that is disruptive, then something will be said or done.

Involvement can be accepting that everyone's contribution can add to the fun or the interest

Many children never discover the value of other people. They may think that someone who is younger isn't worth bothering about. They may make judgements on whether some people are cleverer, more attractive, wealthier, and more fashionable than others, and then make efforts to know only those people who come up to a certain criteria. They may give more respect and attention to those people than they do to people they think are not worth as much. They can miss out on all the contributions that someone they have not rated could have made to their lives. They only want to be involved with the people they rate. This reduces the scope of the involvement that they could have.

Involvement can be giving people time

When children won't give other people a chance and want to have everything their own way, people can feel those children are being unfair. There is only a limited amount of time, even in families, and children need to learn how to share time. Children who don't give others time will not be invited to join activities that depend on people being fair with each other in terms of time. Children who are impatient and find it hard to give other people time often have to give up the activity because they can't bear waiting for their turn.

Involvement can be giving people space

Children who crowd other children and don't allow them space can often feel rejected by the very people they want to be involved with. What they haven't understood is how to be involved in an activity with other children. They think that nearness to another child is all that matters. They don't realise that allowing someone to get on with the activity on their own while they work independently nearby is still companionship.

Some children try and find a friend with whom they can 'twin'. They want to share all aspects of their lives with just one person. They become possessive. If they meet someone happy to be that friend they are lucky but mostly children find that friends will want to do their own thing as well. If this isn't understood then possessive children can feel friendless. Their expectations are unrealistic and at some point there will probably be a falling out. Children who know that people can still like them even if they don't want to be with them all the time will know how to become involved with more people so that they have friends for different activities.

Involvement can be accepting that sometimes the advantage won't be yours

Children who cheat, put other children down, or whinge when things don't go their way become uninvolved for two reasons: they can't stand the pressure that they are putting themselves under and other people can't be bothered coping with someone who is being so unfair. It becomes pointless to play with someone who cheats, who always thinks they should win, or who wrecks the mood by whingeing. It is easier to find someone who enjoys the game for its own sake, sees the humour when things are going wrong and can be pleased when someone else has a success.

Involvement can be knowing that on the law of averages you will get the best opportunities as often as everyone else

Children don't have to compete on a tiny field. If they improve their skills, then they will be picked because they will be needed at some point. They won't know when it is and they might not get the chances somebody else had but there are so many opportunities that they will get the advantage sometimes.

Involvement can mean following up

Following up is a huge part of involvement. It means considering what needs to be done to make the situation successful. A child who knows how to tidy up makes playing with toys an agreeable activity. A child who remembers to hand their homework in makes the doing of the homework worthwhile. A child who says thank you when help has been given or they have been invited somewhere leaves the door open to further help and invitations.

Making the effort to be involved can help children through the door that luck or someone else has opened for them.

Children who are involved might still have a problem but they will be able to show that they are grown up enough to be involved in sorting the problem out.

What to do when your child can't cope because something has gone wrong

You need to be clear when you think about how you are going to help.

Often, you know what you want to say and you know what you want to happen but you are not clear enough in your own mind to be able to explain it to your child. You can improve your chances of getting your child to understand what you mean by thinking things through before you try and explain them to your child. In the long run it may not matter that your explanation wasn't very successful because there will be other opportunities to come back to it.

Practical tips for improving your chances of coming up with a good explanation

Is she having us on?

Peter's daughter sobbed and screamed and refused to get into the water when she went with the school to the swimming pool, but she was happy to go to swimming lessons after school and loved going to the pool at weekends when she could play on the inflatables. A note had come from school to Peter saying that his daughter would not be allowed to go swimming with the school if she carried on being a problem. Peter knew he would have to choose his words carefully if he was going to sort the problem out. His daughter had to know that it was not acceptable for her to behave badly when she went swimming with the school, while managing to behave well when she went swimming at other times.

Tip One – write down the keywords

All the words you write down may not come up in your explanation but you might need to write them down just to get them out of your head. Peter might not tell his daughter that he thinks what she is doing is silly or embarrassing, but since that is what he feels he has to get it off his chest so that it doesn't get in the way when he is trying to think clearly . . .

Peter wrote down these keywords:

- Important
- Co-operate
- Rules
- Water
- Safety
- Fun
- Silliness
- Embarrassment

Tip Two – think about what you want or need your discussion to achieve
Peter wanted his daughter to settle down in the school swimming sessions.

Tip Three – think about how you will know whether your conversation has been understood or not
You might set a target. Peter's target for his daughter might have been that the teacher at school can tell him that his daughter went swimming with no tears.

Tip Four – chat it over with someone else
Talking over a problem often helps you to see whether your thoughts or ideas are clear or muddled.

I don't want to make her life miserable
Donna's mum was telling her friend about the problems Donna was having at school. Donna couldn't concentrate and didn't care that she wasn't finishing her work. As Donna's mum chatted to her friend her friend became confused. Donna's mum seemed to be saying that Donna needed to finish her work but she also seemed to be saying that she wasn't surprised that Donna didn't finish her work because most of the topics didn't really interest her daughter anyway.

So, was she wanting Donna to get her work done, or was she thinking it should be okay for Donna only to finish those pieces of work that she enjoyed doing? When her friend asked what she really wanted, Donna's mum realised she didn't know. Her friend explained she couldn't have it both ways. Either Donna would feel she could do what she wanted when she wanted or she would know that schoolwork mattered and had to be finished. Donna's mum would have to decide.

Tip Five – be clear when you talk to your child
Children will feel demotivated if they don't understand why you are cross with them or why you are taking something so seriously. It is easy for children to pick up the wrong message when you are speaking to them even though what you are saying is perfectly clear to you.

Children can become confused by what you say. You may have:

* Used the wrong words
* Become sidetracked
* Been interrupted
* Forgotten what you were going to say
* Become angry over a side issue
* Made a joke of it
* Given so much positive feedback that the child completely misses the key point of what you are trying to say

Dad's pleased with me

Daniel's son had been rude to his grandmother and something had to be done about it.

Daniel hated it if he felt that he was making his son unhappy. However, he wanted to let his son know that being rude to his grandmother was not acceptable.

He started by saying all the good things that had happened in the afternoon because he didn't want to upset his son. Daniel warmed to his theme. He praised his son for his behaviour in the car, the way he played with his younger cousins and the way he had eaten his roast dinner so nicely, even though Daniel knew that his son hated carrots.

His son listened happily to his father's praise. He was so content at hearing about how well he had done that he really didn't notice the small comment his father finished with, which was about not being rude to his grandmother.

Children can become confused by the way that you say something. You may have:

- Looked away while you were talking
- Smiled while you were talking even though you felt serious
- Said it in a rush while you were busy with something else
- Put your meaning in the wrong form so that your child thinks that doing what you have asked is optional
- Made your request in such a way that your child thinks to do what you have asked will be doing you a favour

Please please me

Jackie had been called up to school several times because Heidi wasn't doing her work. Jackie felt totally intimidated when she went up to school. Schools made her feel as though she was about thirteen-and-a-half, even though she was thirty-eight. She wanted her daughter to get on with her work so that Heidi would get on well with her education, but she didn't say so. She begged Heidi to do the work the teacher asked her to do because, 'mummy gets so upset if she has to go into school'. Heidi wasn't really bothered that her mum didn't like going into school. She saw that as her mum's problem so she didn't see any good reason for getting on with her work.

Ten practical tips for having an important conversation with your child – when you want them to start doing something – and when you want them to stop doing something

1. Make sure you are at the same eye level as your children when you want them to know that you mean what you say.
2. Use a tone of voice that lets your children know you are not playing or being funny. You don't need to shout, but you do need to make it obvious that what you are saying must be listened to.
3. Make sure your children are looking at you when you are speaking. If they look away, insist that they look back before you carry on explaining what you want.
4. Make what you are saying simple. Use short sentences.
5. Don't confuse children by adding in extra bits.
6. Don't think that because your children look upset you must have done something wrong.
7. No matter how amusing the incident might seem, don't laugh. If you feel yourself smiling, turn away until you get control again.
8. If what you are saying is serious, make sure your face is serious, otherwise your children won't understand which message they are supposed to be responding to – the serious words or the smiley face.
9. When you have explained to your children what you want them to do, give them an instruction that is so simple they cannot misunderstand it, e.g. 'Hang up your coat'. Do not say things such as, 'Now be nice' or 'Be a good boy/girl'. These requests are too ambiguous. What is 'nice' to a three-year-old may be totally unacceptable to an adult. Be clear and watch the results.
10. Remind yourself that your children need you to give guidance. You have experience, knowledge and skills and they need to learn from you.

8

Helping the child who has lost his spark

What can cause children to lose their spark?

- Being pushed too early
- Missing the chance to learn something quite vital without anybody realising and therefore being able to provide them with the information that they need to get going again
- Relying on someone else without realising it so that when the person they rely on is not there it is hard to do anything
- Believing that anything they do will be judged unkindly
- Having had a false start and not believing that there is any point in trying again
- Suffering disappointment and being left without guidance
- Somebody else being blamed for them not improving so they aren't given help to get themselves back on track

How can you tell if your child has lost his spark?

Is it only a bit of a hiccup?

Lots of children can suddenly look peaky and strained. For many this can be a short-term condition. They become listless, uninterested and unresponsive. After a few days or a few weeks, they bounce back to being their old selves: they regain their energy, rebalance themselves and resume their happy-go-lucky lives.

It is enough that you stay positive and balanced yourself. Keep an eye on how they are getting on. If they don't bounce back, they may need some help.

Bad days happen to everyone

We can all feel nervous and unsure of ourselves when there has been pressure on us. It can happen after an illness, a holiday, moving house, changing job, taking an exam, filling in a tax return. Sometimes, feelings of unexplained inadequacy wash over us. We can't pin down what has caused us to feel the way we do, we just feel miserable. Children too can be bewildered by the feelings they have.

It seems to be going on a long time

When children don't bounce back, they become apathetic, fractious and withdrawn. In extreme cases, they can become depressed and talk about their overwhelming sense of failure and hopelessness.

The boy who loved his life

At five

Carl at five was a happy child who got on well with both his parents. He was an only child who was settled at school with friends to play with and things he found interesting happening throughout the day. He could easily cope with the pace of his life and the demands made on him. He looked forward to the normal highlights in a child's life – birthday parties, holidays, trips to the cinema, walks with his parents and his favourite bedtime story.

The Downward Spiral

When Carl was six he started to look peaky. His parents thought he was a bit over-tired, so they got him some multivitamins and made sure that he was in bed early.

The first sign that Carl had lost his interest in school was when his teacher started to keep him in over break to finish off his work. It began to happen quite regularly. It was so unlike Carl to find school work a problem. All his basic skills were way above average so it was strange that he was having trouble finishing his work. His parents and his teacher were worried. They thought of the usual reasons for a little boy feeling unhappy:

- Perhaps he was being bullied
- Perhaps he didn't really like his teacher
- Was he worrying about something that was going to happen?

They tried to talk to Carl, but he was unable to help them to help him. He seemed as bewildered as they were about the way he was behaving. He accepted that he must be a naughty boy because he had to stay in at break time but he didn't seem to have the energy to do anything about it. His parents thought he must be being naughty but they couldn't understand why. Perhaps he was doing something wrong that he didn't think was naughty.

Whatever it was, somehow Carl had lost his motivation. The more he fell behind the more he got into trouble and the more depressed he became.

Give some guidance

Carl needed help to find a way of understanding what was going on in his life. He had stopped being involved in his own existence. He was out of touch with himself. He was giving up on everything.

Turning things round

Carl needed help to realise that his feelings were part of life and there would be practical ways of coping with those feelings. Carl's parents talked to him about the ways they cheered themselves up or kept themselves calm when they felt unsure. They asked Carl about the playground because they knew that he got on so well there. They knew he loved playtime and always found something to do or someone to play with.

They asked him what he did when someone didn't want to play with him or thought his idea for a game was silly. They were fascinated when Carl told them that when that kind of thing happened at school and he couldn't think of how to join in he had a favourite tree in the playground. He would go and look for holes in the bark that he thought insects had made.

Carl shows his strengths

Carl's parents were delighted with the conversation they were having with their son. They had never thought of talking to him about how he dealt with life because life up until now had always seemed to go so easily for Carl.

They told him they were thrilled to discover that he had worked out such a successful way of dealing with disappointment. They were pleased that Carl could understand that other people might want to do something without him and didn't feel upset when it happened.

Carl lives his life

Realising Carl had such a mature understanding of social situations meant that finding a way to deal with other parts of his life that weren't going so well could be left up to Carl. Now his parents could offer suggestions to Carl and the chance to talk to them. They told him they felt he was the ideal person to find his own solutions because he was so creative.

Carl gets his spark back

Carl's listlessness disappeared overnight. He became highly motivated to find out what strategy he was going to use that would mean he got his work done. Carl was energised when he discovered just how big a part he could play in his own life. He looked forward to trying different strategies to see what effect they had on the way he did his work.

He tried awarding himself points for each piece of work he had to do; he experimented with taking deep breaths before he started an activity; he investigated which food he could take to have as a snack at playtime; he tried carrot sticks, raisins, cherry tomatoes and cubes of cheese before he settled on sultanas as being his magic power source.

I am interested in me because I want to know what makes me tick

Sometimes children become so interested in the unhappy feelings they have that they are not motivated to let them go.

What is crucial is that children know that when they feel unhappy they know their own ways of making themselves feel better. They need to know how they can get their spark back.

They need to become interested in how they will cope.

Motivating children after a disappointment

After a disappointment children can feel:

- Rejected
- Confused
- Bewildered
- Exhausted
- Guilty
- Unworthy

They can lose their spark.

When there has been a disappointment, children need to draw on their ability to cope.

Children's ability to cope

- For some children coping means being very busy and energised and throwing themselves at anything that is going on.
- Other children prefer to find something quiet to do that does not require a lot of thought. They might find an activity that distracts them.
- Some children are very good at finding a way of coping that isn't going to make the problem worse. They accept that sometimes things in life go easily, sometimes there are hiccups, and sometimes there are outright tragedies. No one else may notice that they are feeling down because they can pick themselves up so quickly.
- For some children the hurt is raw. They have no defences because what has happened was so unexpected that it falls outside any of their coping strategies. These children are likely to make the situation worse. Noisily or quietly they try to justify their need to be distressed.

What can happen when the hurt feels raw

Matthew played tennis in the local club. He and some of his club mates were playing tennis one day when a tennis scout was visiting. They were playing a doubles match and Matthew was playing with his best friend, Chris. Matthew was serving and he was having a brilliant run of play. He was serving deep and returning the ball magnificently. He and Chris were enjoying themselves and Matthew felt great to be on such good form.

That night, Matthew got a call at home asking if he wanted to join another club where the standard was higher. He decided to join because he wanted the challenge. He didn't think about anything else except how proud he was to have been asked. He was stunned when Chris reacted badly.

Chris reacted passionately. He felt Matthew had turned against him. He couldn't stop telling everyone how unfair it was and how Matthew wasn't that good anyway and how he had often beaten him. At first, Chris had other people at the club listening and sort of agreeing but then they weren't interested in talking about Matthew any more. They still saw Matthew and were doing other things with him and continued to enjoy his company. They didn't reject Chris, but Chris rejected anybody who didn't agree with him.

Chris ended up leaving the club and began to hang around with other people who felt life wasn't fair. Having gone from being motivated and excited about tennis, Chris became very negative. He liked to call people losers, swots, sad or any other insult current at the time.

Don't make the situation worse

Chris did not have any coping strategies for disappointment. He had believed that life was always fair and he had a strong belief that he knew what fair was. He decided that it was Matthew's fault that he felt so upset. He couldn't realise that sometimes, one person has the luck to be in the right place at the right time and doing the right thing and that at other times, someone else will have the good fortune. Chris could not be convinced by anyone that Matthew was still living a life like anyone else. Matthew still had to work, make friends, get on with people. His day-to-day life hadn't changed much. Chris couldn't see that. Chris was bitter. He was unable to see Matthew's life realistically at all. He was unable to get on with his own life successfully. He felt overwhelmed and everything was out of proportion.

There is much more to life than disappointment
What happened to Chris is what happens to all of us when we feel that someone else has somehow managed to find a life worth living and all we have found is the dregs.

Everyone has to feel comfortable with who they are before they can be at ease. To do this you have to be generous: you have to be generous to yourself by noticing the efforts you make even if no one else notices them; you have to be generous towards other people and notice their positive qualities; you have to practise noticing your own positive qualities; and you have to know that there are enough chances, love and friendship for everyone.

Other chances will come

If your child has experienced a disappointment:

1. Encourage them to take up other offers or invitations, or find something to laugh at – a video, a film, or a book.
2. Agree that you can feel hurt when you are disappointed.
3. Share with them a time when you felt hurt and did or didn't cope.
4. Look through a photo album together of times they have enjoyed.
5. Tell them that learning how to cope with setbacks is a part of growing up. It isn't really a setback. They haven't gone backwards. It is just that something has changed.

A setback is not a step back

Learning to see that a setback is really just a change helps to create a healthy state of mind. Learning to see others do well and being pleased for them creates a positive environment. Learning to value your own life, even when someone else's seems better, will mean you will take positive steps to enjoy the life you have. Part of enjoying the life you have is taking a proactive role in that life.

To take a proactive role in your life you need to be interested in yourself

You need to discover:

- Who am I?
- What do I actually enjoy doing?
- What sort of people do I like?
- When I look what do I see?
- When I am on my own how do I feel?
- When I am in a big garden what do I like to do?

And so on.

Without knowing yourself you can't make a healthy attachment to others

Children can become dislocated from their own lives for all sorts of reasons – severe illness, separation from parents, a difficult birth, a difficult start to life which has slowed normal development, a change in the family, which could be a new baby, or neglect or abuse – emotional or physical.

What is interesting about me?

You can help children who feel dislocated from their own life and may have no sense that they have a life at all by playing a game of favourites: tell each other what your favourites are. What are your favourite sweets, days of the week, numbers, colours, places, smells, foods, television programmes, stories, characters from books, items of clothing, animals, drinks, things to play on in the park, places to sit.

You don't have to question the child further about what they have said, just let them feel comfortable with the idea that they are entitled to have favourites.

Who am I?

Liam seemed very cut off from his own world or anybody else's world. He didn't seem to have a spark. He didn't seem interested in his own life or anyone else's. At four, he would prefer to sit outside the group, facing away from the others and finding something to play with on his own. He didn't look at other children or answer to his own name. He was fixated on different things but the motivation for doing them seemed completely random to an observer and this made it difficult for an adult or other children to capitalise on Liam's interest and use it to help him move forward.

How to help a child who has never had the spark

Begin by sitting next to him while he is playing. He might be interested in your presence or he might not. While you sit alongside him, write sentences that start with his name. Read aloud as you write.

Liam's sentences

Liam is a boy.
Liam is four.
Liam has got red shorts.

Liam became interested in the sentences and would sit alongside the person writing them. He would answer questions about what he had eaten for breakfast and the information would be included in the sentences: *Liam had toast and butter for breakfast.*

Over several months, Liam began repeating the sentences after they were read out to him. He would take his sentences round to show other people what they said. He could still tell people what the sentences said a couple of hours later. He became motivated to suggest ideas for sentences because he now wanted to please the other people who he could 'read' them to. Everyone was motivated to work at developing Liam's interest in himself and in other people.

Liam became a vibrant member of any group. He knew who he was. He was fascinated to find out who other people were. The sort of activities Liam began to enjoy were ones where children shared their likes and dislikes or told each other bits of information about themselves.

The fundamentals of helping a child who has lost the spark are:

- Help them to relax
- Help them to be happy with who they are
- Help them to know there will be other opportunities
- Help them to know they will be able to cope
- Help them to know that tomorrow is another day

9

Helping the child
who gives up

What makes some children give up?

- They don't see an end
- They don't know how to get to an end
- They have no confidence that the end they are pursuing is the one they should be pursuing
- They don't know who to ask for help
- They think the next thing might be hard
- They don't know how to pace themselves
- They don't believe they are good enough to finish
- They don't know how to get to the end
- They have parents who think it's too hard for them
- They have parents who give up
- They will only do it with support

Often, when children give up, they know they have been defeated by something quite small. Because they don't see themselves as able to solve the small problem they add in all sorts of other reasons for giving up. They hope these reasons will help adults to understand just how necessary it is that they give up. It is difficult to help children when they do this. Whenever a suggestion is made or advice is given, children who have given up will come up with a whole stack of reasons why having another go or starting again is impossible. They won't look for a way to keep going.

Looking for a way to keep going

Joanna had homework to do. She had forgotten to bring her homework diary home so she rang her friend to find out what it was she had to do. The idea of giving up didn't enter her head. If she didn't know what the homework was, she would ring her friend; if her friend had forgotten, then she would ring Joanna.

Looking for a reason to give up

Paul had homework to do. He had a hangdog expression because he hadn't brought his homework diary home. He couldn't remember what they had been doing at school. When he looked in his exercise book, it didn't give him any clues as to what he was meant to do. He couldn't think of anyone he could phone. He thought most of his friends would be out and anyway he didn't think they would know either. When his dad suggested he do some notes on the subject that he could take in instead of his homework, Paul said he had lost his pencil-case. Paul knew that in the end if he came up with enough reasons for not doing his homework, his parents would give up as well.

The truth is that when someone perfects the art of giving up, they actually convince themselves that giving up is the only option.

What is the fallback position?

Joanna had a fallback position. She had a friend to ring. She had spare pencils and pens. So did Paul. It was just that Paul couldn't see that instead of giving up he should use whatever he had to get on with whatever he could.

Seeking out a solution

Sanjay went to karate classes on a Wednesday evening after school. He loved the sessions and was getting on very well. He got himself to the classes, which were straight after school, and then his mum would pick him up on her way home from work.

The karate teacher had to change the lesson evening to a Thursday and told her pupils. This was a problem for Sanjay, because his mum always worked late on a Thursday. There would be no one to him pick him up. It looked like he wouldn't be able to keep doing karate. A few days later, Sanjay came home from school and said he had found someone else who went to karate whose dad would be able to give him a lift home. He had this boy's phone number so his mum could ring to check that the arrangement was OK. Sanjay had it sorted.

Stopping at a setback

Jasmine was good at basketball and was in the team at school. One afternoon her P.E. teacher handed out leaflets about a new basketball club that was starting up at the leisure centre. As soon as Jasmine saw what night the sessions were on, she said she couldn't go. Her mum didn't have the car that night and there was no other way she could get there. Her P.E. teacher was disappointed as she thought Jasmine would get a lot out of being in the club, but Jasmine was so definite that she wouldn't be able to get there that her teacher didn't try to change her mind or suggest ways round the problem.

What needs sorting?

Sanjay knew that he needed a way to get home from the class on a Thursday. With this in mind he found what he needed. Sanjay had a solution in mind and he found it.

Jasmine knew that her mum wouldn't have the car. With this in mind she would never find what she needed. Jasmine had the problem in mind. End of story.

If you want to help your children to be motivated to keep going rather than give up, encourage them to think in terms of fallback positions and what needs sorting.

What if sorting it out is beyond them?

Alicia started secondary school and in the first week was in trouble because she didn't do her homework. She didn't do her homework because she didn't understand how to do it. Alicia didn't tell her mother that she had homework, she just didn't do it. She felt her mother had no time to help her with her homework because she was so busy.

When she got into trouble, Alicia was horrified and said she felt too ill to go to school. Her mum took her to the doctor and Alicia had two days 'off sick'.

Alicia was dreading going back to school because she knew there would be more homework and she had no idea how she was going to do it. She said she was sick again.

Her aunt came to sit with her while her mum was at work. Her aunt had an idea that Alicia wasn't really sick and there was another reason why she didn't want to go to school. Alicia told her aunt about the homework problem and her aunt said that Alicia must always do her homework. Alicia burst into tears and said she couldn't ask her mum for help because her mum was busy.

Helping Alicia become motivated to get her homework done

Alicia's aunt came up with a solution. She could go to her aunt's house twice a week and her aunt would help her get the homework done. Alicia suddenly became motivated to do her homework. There was never any trouble about Alicia turning up. She was always highly motivated to get her homework done. Alicia found she didn't need as much help as she had thought she was going to. She heard about a homework club at school that she could go to at lunchtimes. She became highly motivated to have the homework right, done on time, and handed in.

Overwhelmed, not unmotivated

Alicia had been overwhelmed by her situation. That was why she wanted to give up. She felt she wasn't up to the challenge and had no one to turn to who could help her. Alicia's aunt saw that Alicia was floundering and thought it was beyond her niece to sort out the problem by herself. She needed some support. Alicia didn't need much support before she got back on track. The support was having her aunt to talk to and a place to go to where she could do her homework when it was making her feel like she had to give up.

Helping Alicia become motivated to do her homework herself

For the first couple of weeks everything was fine. Alicia's aunt was pleased to see her niece's eagerness, concentration and commitment to her homework. She didn't mind giving Alicia a lot of help, or even giving her the answers, in some cases, because Alicia had so much to catch up on she needed that support. Then Alicia's progress faltered. As the weeks went by, it became clear that Alicia had not understood that she needed to build on her skills so she could do more and more of her own homework.

Unintentionally, Alicia had picked up the idea that her aunt would always give her the answer. Alicia thought this was part of her relationship with her aunt. Alicia would often read out the question to her aunt, pick up her pen ready to write and then do nothing other than look encouragingly at her aunt. It was as if she were a secretary waiting for dictation. Her aunt couldn't understand what was going on. She became angry and wished she had never offered to help with Alicia's homework. She had thought she was going to be a springboard for Alicia, but she had been turned into Alicia's drudge. For a couple of sessions there was some friction while new ground rules were laid. She realised that there had to be an adjustment.

The ground rules were:

- That Alicia would do as much as she could on scrap paper
- Her aunt would check the work that Alicia had done and make suggestions
- Alicia would follow up the suggestions and make the corrections and then copy the work out

If someone starts to slide back after you have given them help, don't feel all is lost. Try not to think that you are back to square one. When helping anybody you may need to continually make adjustments so that they can keep moving forward.

Support plus sympathy led to self-reliance

Alicia could have become totally demotivated. She could have been demotivated when she arrived at secondary school and was given work that was too difficult. She could have been demotivated when her aunt got cross. What kept her motivation high was that an adult, her aunt, offered help bridge the gap between Alicia not being able to do something and being able to do it. The first bridge was between having no homework to hand in and getting the homework done. The second was from having her aunt do the homework to having her aunt's support to do the homework. The next bridge would be from Alicia needing support for all her homework to Alicia recognising the homework tasks that she could do on her own, without help and to a high standard.

Bridging the gap

See giving help as making a series of bridges that lead your children from the place where they have got stuck to the next place that they may be able to manage on their own. Keep watching, so that you are ready to make another bridge when it is needed.

The boy who couldn't find the piece

Daniel had had a very tough beginning. His parents were both drug addicts and he had suffered a lot of neglect before his grandparents were able to have him to live with them. He could barely speak at seven and found it very difficult to concentrate on anything at all.

His grandparents and aunts and uncles worked with him and loved him. Daniel's speech began to improve and he was delighted to find he had a voice and people were interested in what he could say.

What he couldn't do was handle any school work. He could not hold enough information in his mind to be able to work on his own at all. He was not motivated because he couldn't see how to start. When he did a jigsaw, he would just move the pieces around the floor. Even simple jigsaws were too difficult. His gran decided to teach him through jigsaws.

Teaching through jigsaws

First, she asked him what he could see. She would wait until he gave her an answer. Often he would look as though he hadn't heard the question, and she would ask him to repeat the question. If he had forgotten it, she would say the question again. She would ask Daniel to tell her what he was going to do next. A thirty-piece jigsaw might take an hour to complete. All the time Daniel's gran would be asking questions so Daniel would learn to have an idea in his mind when he was looking at the pieces.

Ideas Daniel had to keep in his mind

- What colour was he looking for?
- What shape was he looking for?
- Was he looking for a side piece, a top piece, or a bottom piece?
- Had he checked the picture on the box?
- Do pieces around the edge have joining pieces sticking out?

Keeping ideas in mind

We all have ideas in our minds about our life that help us organise what we have to do:

- I wash my face when I wake up

- I put my shoes near the front door
- I feed the cat before breakfast

I've no ideas at all

Children who have suffered neglect can miss the vital stage of learning how ideas will help them to organise their lives.

As Daniel was told each piece of information, he was getting a chance to build up a storehouse of questions that would help him organise the way to do a jigsaw.

He was able to hear questions in school differently. He could see that he could ask himself questions that would help him get started. It took several years before Daniel could catch up with his age group. Lack of stimulus and expectations when children are young can mean that they really have no idea how to motivate themselves without careful, patient and long-term help.

Children who have suffered crises

One of the myths to which parents cling when they are dealing with a crisis is that the children will be too young or too old to be affected. They believe that if children are given counselling or treats or that the crisis is not mentioned, children will be fine. This is not the case, but it is possible to provide children with support so that they can cope with the changes that crises bring.

Be sympathetic not simply pathetic

Children need support, not wrapping in cotton wool. Crises concerning birth, death, separation, loss, sex, love, harassment, friendship, family and bullying are all part of life. Crises often involve us in fundamental changes. We might change where we live, with whom we live, how we live, or how we think. Children need to learn how to be involved in that process of change, otherwise they will give up. They will lose their identity. They won't feel involved and they won't expect to become involved.

Communication is the key

Children need to be kept informed. They need to be kept in the loop. They need to be able to express all the feelings they have. They need to be able to say that they think things should be done differently. They need to know some situations are beyond their control and be helped to understand how to feel effective when they feel powerless.

Adults can feel that children shouldn't have to cope with anything that is hard. In fact what often happens is that the things that adults define as being too hard for children to deal with are the things that adults find hard to explain. Sometimes children can understand exactly what is going on. They may not see it in the same terms as the adults and the adults may not want to hear.

Permission to think means they won't give up

It is important for us to realise that if we avoid talking about crises with children then children can find it hard to grow up. They have no framework, vocabulary, knowledge or permission to think about, talk about or come to terms with the day-to-day difficulties or changes which are part of everybody's life.

Children left with no way of communicating can become vulnerable. This vulnerability may show itself in a variety of ways. Children may become passive or retreat in order to survive, or they may become aggressive or depressed because they have no other way of expressing the effect the change is having on them.

Give them the words

If children are not given the framework, vocabulary, knowledge and permission to talk about what is happening to them, then their development is left in their own hands. Leaving children without a structure in a crisis can have disastrous or depressing consequences. But don't despair if you think this might have happened.

There will be another time

All is not lost. There will be other opportunities to talk about the crisis and help the child find a framework to make sense of his feelings. It may happen when the child is older. It may happen when there is a distance between the event and the present. The starkness of the events and the rawness of the emotions may have been gradually reduced so that communication can be easier to handle.

Many of us have friends whose lives are in turmoil. It may be temporary turmoil but it is obvious their children are affected. Some parents do not want to admit that they are not in control. They are so scared about the crisis that their mind has gone numb. The one time that most people would like to feel in control is when a crisis happens. If they can't be perfectly at ease when a crisis happens many people would rather pretend that no crisis is happening. This is hard on children.

It is essential to realise that parents are not always able to be responsible for everything they do or don't do, know or don't know. Most parents will meet a time when they are almost totally dependent on other people to support them while their family is going through a crisis, and most parents will be aware of times when they are important in their friends' lives, able to offer practical help, words of support, wisdom and encouragement which their friends cannot find for themselves.

Some guidelines

Since crises are a part of everybody's life many responsible parents want to provide opportunities for their children to explore the range of feelings and actions that are possible in a crisis. This way parents feel they are providing some framework, vocabulary, knowledge and experience that their children can draw on in the future.

What you want in the end is to have helped your children reach adulthood, able to:

- Listen
- Learn

- Share
- Risk
- Question
- Reflect on the impact they have on the world around them

You also want them to know how the world around impacts on them.

There is a balance between protecting children and giving them an insight into the difficulties life can throw up. Sometimes we get it right and at others we don't. Sometimes it seems to be going wrong and then we can get it right.

Some plans go wrong

Sarah wanted Jessica to learn about vulnerability. As an only child, Jessica seemed to be living a charmed life. She had never been seriously ill, never needed emergency treatment at the hospital, everyone around her was fit, healthy and full of life. There was no one in Jessica's life whom Jessica could help. There was no one who was vulnerable. Sarah thought that getting a pet would be a good way to introduce her daughter to the responsibility of caring for something that was vulnerable. Jessica would need to feed the cat, groom it and clean up after it.

Sarah had a lovely picture in her mind of the cat and Jessica becoming inseparable buddies, loving and being loved by each other. Mother and daughter bought the food bowl and the basket and got to know the cat. Jessica couldn't wait for the cat to be allowed out and felt very kind and very responsible when the cat-flap was installed so that the cat could come and go as it pleased.

Imagine Sarah's horror when she found that the first time the cat used the cat flap it dragged through a very dead robin. Sarah's heart sank further as she realised that this could be the robin that hopped about on their patio pecking at the toast Jessica saved for it each morning. This wasn't what Sarah had planned. How was she going to explain all this to Jessica? Should she dump the remains of the bird in the bin and pretend that it had never happened? Should she leave the robin where it was and see what Jessica would do when she came in? Should she give the cat away? Before she had time to reach for the phone and ask her own mum what to do, Jessica skipped into the kitchen.

I don't care! I don't want it now
Jessica went from horrified to devastated to distraught in a matter of seconds. She was horrified at the bloody mess on the floor, devastated that her beloved cat had killed a bird and distraught when she realised it was the bird she considered a special friend in the garden.

In a split second all Sarah's plans to teach Jessica how to care for a vulnerable creature fell apart. To Jessica her cat had become a monster. It was out of control. She didn't want it in the house and anyway, how could it be vulnerable if it could kill things?

Now what do I do?
Sarah felt completely at sea. Her adult plan was a mess. Sarah felt like shouting at Jessica because she felt so disappointed and she also felt like getting rid of the cat and never having another pet. She wanted everything ship-shape and tidy and her world to be filled with only nice things.

To Jessica it was quite simple. She wanted to bury the bird with a full funeral and she wanted the cat locked up in the laundry.

All is not lost
Sarah realised there was another lesson that she could help Jessica to understand, and it wasn't the lesson she was anticipating when she bought a fluffy cat. She had bought the cat because she wanted to help Jessica to deal with things that were vulnerable in a positive way. She could still do that. Jessica could benefit from this incident. She could learn that many things which happen in life don't go as we plan them. Creatures which seem vulnerable in one situation can be dangerous in another. Few situations are black and white, and even fewer situations can be dealt with as if they are black and white.

Part of growing up is being helped to realise that most crises fall into a sort of a grey area. The blackness is softened by the whiteness.

Over the next couple of days, Jessica and her mum talked about the good things and the bad things to do with owning a cat.

There are some situations which are very clear and there are some situations which are not.

When situations are very complicated you will be feeling your way. This can be bad enough when it is only you who is involved. It is a lot worse when you are trying to help your child. The important thing is to find something positive and to avoid giving up.

10

Helping the child who won't work with you

Why children won't work with you

Children may not work with you because:

- They have no experience of working with you on something hard
- They think that parents are different from teachers and home should be quite separate from school
- They always feel frustrated because you don't help them in the way they find helpful
- You haven't really got the time to sit down and work with them so you feel under pressure and so do they every time you do try to help them
- There are too many distractions in the house for anyone who hasn't learned how to focus
- You may not have realised how important it is for you to model what you are trying to get them to do

Protect time to plan

If your child will work with other people yet won't work with you, you need to seriously consider what you have been doing. Think about whether you need to adjust your timetable or your child's timetable. Think about whether there is something else that needs adjusting.

Find ways to help

Children can feel too tired, too stressed, too ignorant, too distracted, too stale or too incompetent to have a go with you. There are ways you can help them to feel energetic, relaxed, optimistic, refreshed and capable so that they will enjoy working with you, and anyone else.

Too tired?

Olivia's parents wanted to make sure that there was a clear difference between the school day and her home life. They were very happy to help Olivia to do the homework that the school had set but felt she should have some time to recover from school before she got on and did the homework.

Olivia was seven and she looked forward to the time between school and bed. She liked school and was doing well but when it was time to do her homework she would whinge. Her parents would shout and threaten to take away privileges. Olivia would always promise that tonight when it came to time to do her homework she would get on with it without complaining. Somehow she never did.

Her parents tried bribery: if Olivia could get on and do her homework without moaning she could have a treat. Olivia never got the treat because when it came to it she resisted doing her work all the same. She would argue about doing her homework for hours.

There will never be time

Olivia wanted to join the Brownies but when her mum followed up Olivia's request, she found that the meetings didn't finish until seven o'clock. She felt sure that by the time Olivia was picked up there would be no time to do any homework before bed.

Olivia's mum put the problem, as she saw it, to Olivia. She explained to Olivia that Brownies couldn't really be fitted in with Olivia's free time after school and getting her homework done. Olivia promised that she would do her homework as soon as she got home if that would mean she could go to Brownies. Olivia's mum was sure this wouldn't work in the long term. Surely the whole evening would be spent with Olivia arguing about whether she should do her homework, how much she was to do and how well it was to be done. They would never get to Brownies.

Olivia's mum was surprised to find that on the day of her first Brownie meeting, Olivia rushed in, got out her books and got on with gusto. She thought this was just a 'one off'. She was very surprised to find that every Thursday evening Olivia did the same thing.

If you can do it on Brownies night, why not all the time?

Olivia still baulked at homework on every other night of the week but Thursdays were different. Her mum and dad felt upset. They began to view Olivia with caution. They started to see her as someone who would only do things when it suited her. Olivia wanted to go to Brownies so she got on with her homework affably – on that night. They began to feel as if they were being manipulated and they didn't like it. They had to feel that they were still in charge. They explained to her how they felt and said she would have to do all her work each night.

We don't always know everything

It isn't unusual for parents to build up a belief about their children that is wrongly based. Sometimes that belief is positive but many times it is negative because parents are so anxious that their children respond in the way that they think all children should. If their child doesn't behave in the way they feel children should, they become nervous as parents and feel as if they are getting everything wrong.

Often all it takes is for the parents to have a closer look around at the way other families organise themselves. Then they can see that there are lots of different ways of reaching the same end result. They stop feeling so panic-stricken that the way they imagined things would happen hasn't actually come about and they start looking for alternatives.

Remember you are creating your family life. Often there are no rights and wrongs, it is just what fits in for the whole family and the individuals who make up that family.

Have a closer look

What could have happened here is that Olivia's parents had completely misread the situation. Olivia might have always been happy to do her homework after school, every night. Then she could relax and know that there would be no more demands made on her until the next morning.

It could have happened that the first type of homework Olivia got from school was listening to a story read to her by her mum or dad and then talking with them about the pictures. This was a lovely pre-bed activity and it fitted in really well with the way the family wanted to spend their evenings. As Olivia carried on at school the homework tasks had changed. Now she had to do a bit of writing, learn a few spellings, or complete a maths worksheet. It was no longer the sort of thing the family could cuddle up with together on the bed, yet they were still trying to do it at the same time – just before bed.

It could have been that Olivia was just too tired by the end of the day to cope with the intellectual demands of homework at that time of night. It could even be that as far as school work was concerned, Olivia was a morning person and not an evening person.

Staying in charge

What must be remembered is that it is best when things are going wrong to believe that those involved really want things to go well. You do and your child does. Try different solutions to see if they work. If they don't work, keep thinking. If they do work, don't believe that things will always stay the same. As the child grows up, as the family gets bigger, as demands change, new ways of coping with the situation will be needed.

Don't panic when something that has worked well for many weeks, months or years starts to unravel. It is just time for a change. You will need to reassess what is happening and what needs to happen. Involve your children in these processes because then they will become adept at working out how to get motivated and stay motivated themselves whatever is happening.

Some solutions
- If your children want to talk instead of working, stop the work and try this exercise: the children and you can sit up straight with feet on the floor and count down from ten. Do this slowly. Alternatively, the children can put their heads on the table and count down from ten.
- Explain why quiet is essential for thought. Do an experiment. How long does it take to do the work when there is quiet compared to when there is chatting?
- Use a timer. Tell your children everyone is to be quiet for one minute while they work. Choose a small stretch of time because most children will be able to be quiet for that time. When you are sitting quietly you will be giving them a good example. It is easier for children to understand how to be still if they see you do it.
- Talk about homework as a chance to practise school work, but also as a chance to learn self-control. Let children know they have choices about the way they approach something. To be in a bad temper about having to do homework is a choice. It is not something that has to happen just because there is homework to be done.

Too stressed?

Georgina is ten and has exceptional abilities in creative writing. She is very co-operative at school but often tense. She is competitive but despairs if she doesn't think she is the best. She has friends and is never unpleasant to other people who she thinks are doing better than she is. However, when she gets home, her tension becomes anger and, in some cases, aggression. She refuses to do anything with her parents and they find they have to be very firm. Georgina doesn't want to show them her homework and she won't make any of the corrections that they suggest. Life is a battle because every school day includes set homework. It could be that:

- Georgina feels her parents criticise too much
- Georgina's parents forget to praise her for what she has done well and only draw attention to what she has done badly
- Her parents might be so stressed themselves that Georgina can't bear to deal with them at all because she can't cope with how stressed she gets
- Georgina could feel that the whole thing is unfair – she has worked hard throughout the day and wants her home life to be more free and easy
- Georgina can't think what to do to make it better

Some solutions
If you want to de-stress your children:

- Tell them when they are doing something well.
- Make sure that you don't prize only things that they have done at school and got good marks for. Keep things they have found. The feather that they picked up on a walk could be stuck on the fridge for a couple of weeks or they could cut out a joke they thought was really funny from a comic. Help them see aspects of life that are worth valuing but don't get marked.
- Encourage them to start a collection of something like post-

cards. They will see the pleasure that they can get from things other than getting ten out of ten. It could be pictures of dogs or different key rings but it is something for them to be interested in, absorbed by, and not competing over.

Work on yourself so your child will work with you: life is more than school

To break into this cycle of stress and self-preservation on the part of your child, you need to think of imaginative ways and places where homework can be done. Think of different ways of asking about the school day. Instead of focusing on marks, who came top, who finished first and who got praise from the teacher, the conversation can be about something trivial that has nothing to do with school and makes a break and allows the attention to settle on other areas. If this is too hard try a joke book and take it in turns to read out or tell jokes.

Too ignorant?

Mark resisted working with his mum because he liked her to see him as a clever little boy, but every time she tried to help him with his homework she asked questions that Mark couldn't answer. He was used to telling her the things he could do. She was always happy to hear how well he was getting on. He would rush in from the garden to tell her he had kept the ball up in the air for longer than ever before. She would praise him and he would race off to try and keep the ball up even longer. When he had homework to do it was quite different. Mark didn't want his mum to know that he couldn't do all his spellings. He didn't want her to see the mistakes in his maths book. He felt she wouldn't think he was clever if she knew he was getting things wrong.

Some solutions
* If you have a child like Mark you can help by turning him into your teacher. If he has some spelling to do get him to tell you which words are easy and which are difficult.

- Make a notice saying, 'Silent Working' or 'Great Brains Thinking', and stand it on the table.
- Ask your child how he is going to tackle the difficult words. If he has no ideas, tell him what you would do but don't tell him that is what he must do. You want to encourage him to think about possibilities. If you can work with children in this way, you will be amazed at how the children will keep thinking for themselves because they will feel that you are interested in listening to their thoughts in the same way as before you were interested in their successes.
- If children make a mistake when they have spelt the word for you, help them work out what went wrong. Don't tell them what was wrong. Get them to look with you or on their own at their list of spellings so that they can spot the mistake for themselves.
- Affirm the bits that have been done correctly. Try and keep yourself as an interested and enthusiastic listener rather than an instructor.

Too distracted?

Andy's parents were frustrated by his lack of concentration. Andy hated doing any work at home. His teachers said that he didn't concentrate at school. He was in the second groups so most of his work was average or above average but his parents wanted him to be in the top groups. Andy was always fiddling with something. He was his parents' first child. They felt education was important and something had to be done.

Some solutions
- If you can stop the fiddling you will help create calm. Calmly remove the thing that is being fiddled with or keep moving the child's hand away from what he is touching.
- Break off the activity and do some finger exercises to release tension. Finish by shaking the hands as if you are trying to shake off drips of water.

- Staying still is extremely important if you want to create calm and optimism. Whenever children are agitated, get them to stand with their feet on the floor, hands by their sides and take some deep breaths until they feel they are back in control of themselves.

Too impulsive?

Jenny was a lively, sociable little girl who could organise anybody and any event. She was fascinated by people and was very positive with all the people she came into contact with. There was a complete character change when Jenny came to do homework. She would whinge, shout, flounce and sob. Her mum and step-dad dreaded homework time. It could go on for hours. Jenny would guess wildly whenever she was supposed to be coming up with an answer. Her parents had done most of the homework that was taken back to school. Jenny's parents were very concerned because it was obvious that they were being manipulated but they had no idea what they should do.

Some solutions

- To get over the problem of guessing wildly insist on the child waiting a minute before he gives an answer.
- Ask what sort of an answer he is thinking of giving. Is it going to be a word, a number, a sentence or a name? By doing this the child can get some structure in his thinking before he gives an answer.
- Ask a question that your child can answer to build his confidence and his belief that questions can be answered.
- Let him know that a wrong answer is OK. A wrong answer gives you information about what you and your child need to do next. A thoughtful answer, even if it is wrong, is very helpful.

Too stale?

Nicholas had been trying for many months to improve his reading. It seemed impossible for him to make any progress. Sometimes his parents felt that it was not a case of one step forward, two steps back, but more a case of three steps back always, and only occasionally one step forward.

Nicholas was fed up. He was a 'good' child. He didn't complain but he didn't seem to put anything into his reading. His dad knew he had intelligence because he had seen how quickly his son could learn if he wanted to know something.

When children are stale the problem can be that they make you feel stale as well. You have to let them find some way of freshening up what is going on. Share with your children that working with them is boring for you and boring for them. See how you can pep up homework time.

Some solutions
- Open the window to get some fresh air
- Do some exercises together. These can be scrunching your face, stretching arms in the air, shrugging your shoulders
- Have a sip of water
- Go outside and run up and down on the spot
- Sing a song and move with the rhythm

Deciding to get a tutor because your children won't work with you

You might have tried everything you can think of and it is still not working. You might decide to get a tutor.

Tutors

How a tutor can motivate children when parents can't
When children go to a tutor the parents are paying for someone to find a way to:

- Help the children take responsibility for their own work
- Show children how to find information for themselves
- Teach children several important skills

Tutors have:

- Knowledge about what it is reasonable to expect from a child of that age
- Expertise in how to help a child to gain the knowledge they need and use the knowledge they have
- Time set aside for this one activity
- One role only and that is to help the child with their learning

Parents have:

- Limited experience of children of a certain age and so often aren't sure what it is reasonable to expect from a child at a particular age
- Expertise in their own field that may not be teaching. Teachers are specialists and sometimes parents need specialist help, although at other times they don't
- So many demands on their time. Children can often work out how to delay or waste the limited time that is available for them
- Nurturing, teaching, housekeeping and earning roles to name just a few

Have at least one aim

If you decide that the best course of action is to get a tutor for your children because they aren't motivated to work with you and you can't get them to be motivated, decide what your aim is and let the tutor know. Your aim may be to have your children do their work at home with you without a fuss. The tutor will then know what information you need about how your aim can be achieved.

Sometimes parents stop the tuition as soon as their children have started to get on with their work in a sensible way or as soon as they have moved up groups at school. It looks like the problem has been solved and everyone feels as though the children are back on track.

It can happen that the children are fine for a few weeks but then seem to slip back into their old behaviours. If this happens to you, don't feel that all is lost or that what you have done has been wasted. Either build in some extra time to get homework done or ask for a couple of extra tuition sessions.

Don't let the situation slide back so that the old habits really get a grip. Tuition helps to remind everyone how to overcome difficulties and move forward.

The fundamentals when you are choosing a tutor are:

- Have your aim
- Share that aim with the tutor and the child
- Try and establish what the tutor thinks the child needs
- Change your aim if that seems sensible
- Keep alert and be ready to help if the child begins to falter

Why aren't you my dream child?

- I can't understand why my child doesn't enjoy reading in the way that I did
- I always had a book in my hand
- I can remember when I was little, I loved reading. It didn't matter what I read, I always had at least two books on the go. I can't remember not being able to read. I got comics, books as presents, joined the library as early as I could, and read my older sister's books

This is not so much a case of wanting your child to work with you as wanting your child to be a clone of you.

The danger of worrying that your child isn't exactly like you were is:

- You may have a false memory
- You may have done it once or twice but now you look back you think you behaved like that all the time
- You may be missing the special bits that make your child different to you

135

- You are frightened to let your child be human, you are expecting perfection
- You are undermining your own self-esteem as a parent

Be realistic if you want your child to work with you

A real child is great fun and a great challenge. You can't control how your child learns or works because it will be their own way of processing the information around them. What you can control are the opportunities. Parents want their children to have opportunities. It is important that parents see that studying, doing homework, revising, going to Cubs or visiting grandma are all opportunities for their children. As adults, parents have to prioritise the opportunities.

Spot the opportunity

Nicky was married with two children. She saw her own parents every fortnight. She would either take the family there or her parents would come to her house. They had lunch together and then Nicky chatted to her mum and dad for a couple of hours. Her parents were creatures of habit and the afternoons always followed the same pattern: lunch and then a cup of tea and a chat.

As Nicky's children grew older, all the adults found a way to make the visits to or from the grandparents something that was positive. The children had started to ask if they could do something else but Nicky felt it was important that they have some contact with their grandparents.

The solution was that when the grandparents came to their house, the children could get their homework done after lunch. This worked really well. The grandparents felt they were still involved in their grandchildren's lives. The children felt a sense of belonging and that they were making the most of what was happening.

The children did try to sort out homework to take with them when they went to their grandparents' house but that didn't work out as well. They often forgot something vital and then sat there looking worried or fed up for the rest of the afternoon. The grandparents had the idea that the children could take a video. They could record something in the week to take with them. This worked really well. They never forgot to set the video and they always remembered to take it with them. They looked forward to the visits and so did everyone else. Adults and children had made the most of the opportunities.

What is the opportunity for?

Cheryl's house was fraught for the people who lived there and a delight for the people who visited. Cheryl loved to take any opportunity. Friends would drop in for drinks and be encouraged to stay for tea. People always stayed much longer than they thought they were going to. It was such a friendly house and the welcome was so warm and genuine.

Cheryl's children had to fit in around this. They took the opportunities they thought Cheryl approved of. They showed guests their bedrooms or some new toy. They were friendly and helpful. They loved to chat and were very sociable. They were bathed in approval from everyone who visited. When people left, the children would flop on the settee, pleased to have the house back to themselves and tired from their playing and entertaining.

Once the washing up was finished, Cheryl would ask the children about homework, P.E. kit, spelling lists and notes for school. The children became defensive, argumentative and distressed.

Why had this happened?
No opportunity had been provided or allowed for them to sort out what they needed to for school. Now they were being shouted at for not having done something that they couldn't see they had had any time to do. This went on week after week for years. Cheryl was taking and making the most of social opportunities. Every-

thing could be dropped for the chance for the family to be with friends, go on a walk or have a bike ride.

Cheryl hadn't realised she had to provide opportunities for the children to get their homework done, pack their bags and sort out what they needed to do for school. She had learned how to be organised. As the adult, she was in control of the time. She didn't realise the agitation, distress and powerlessness that her children felt over organising their own lives. They just didn't know how to do it. There had been no space or opportunity for them to learn.

Teaching how to take an opportunity is time well spent

Philippa's house was full of activity. Her children had the opportunity to have friends round but Philippa also arranged times to see her own friends. When children visited they would have the opportunity to dress up, chat, make dens, help with cooking, do some art and craft, put on music and have a disco. Philippa's children knew that if they organised what they had to do – feeding the hamster, tidying their rooms, doing their homework and their other activities – then, if there was a beautiful day, they would be able to take the opportunity to do something spontaneous. Philippa gave her children lots of opportunities to learn how to take responsibility. They knew what to do. They would offer to entertain a visitor by reading their reading book to them. They would happily ask people to test them on their spellings. They were delightful and spontaneous children.

Making the most of the opportunities

1. Talk about what is going to happen next. If it is a four-hour drive to the campsite, talk about what the opportunities will be for the journey:
   * Reading a book
   * Telling jokes
   * Collecting number plates

- Having a sleep
- Listening to story tapes
- Singing
- Planning the menu
- Planning trips

2. Get the children to sort out what they need to take with them for the journey. They could have a bag or a box into which they put what they need especially for the journey. Don't 'pooh-pooh' outlandish suggestions, ask instead what they will put in the bag to make sure they have something to do.

    This preparation can work for other outings too.

3. If it is a sudden invitation, outline with your children a quick list of what needs to be done in order to accept the invitation. Don't start running around on your own making sure that everyone can get out of the door. Involve the children. Get them to put out extra water for the cat, push a note through next door, or make any of the phone calls that have to be made. Let them help to make the most of the opportunity. Let them see what has to be done in order to make the most of the opportunity.

4. Help your children keep an eye open for opportunities. There will be half an hour before tea is ready – is that a good time to practise skipping? There is still some water in the paddling pool – what could that go on? There is some pastry left from making the pie – what do they want to use it for? Their favourite programme doesn't start for another ten minutes – how about doing the title for their homework?

    It doesn't matter what it is or how it is used. It can be time, it can be materials, it can be space, it can be interest. What you want children to do is see the opportunity that is there and think about the possibility of using it.

5. Letting an opportunity pass. It is very important to know that sometimes you make the most of your opportunities by saying

no to something that is suggested. You may think that your child is too young, has too much to do, you don't have the money, you don't have the time, it's not an experience which you feel is important, it may not be safe.

Even if your friends or your children's friends put pressure on you to say yes, you must feel that part of making the most of opportunities is knowing that you can be selective. One of the best things that you can teach your children is that no can be a reasonable thing to say.

Saying 'yes' or 'no' both have consequences, but 'no' is just as full as 'yes'. If children think they always have to say yes to an opportunity they can get into difficulty when they have to make decisions when you are not there.

'No' doesn't mean that you dislike people or that you are negative. It doesn't mean that you are a loser, a wimp, or that you always say no. Your children are not always responsible for making their friends happy. It is important that children feel they can be autonomous when it is appropriate. They too can make decisions based on what they think is right at the time.

Blocks of time

Adults often think in blocks of time: half an hour to get tea ready; fifteen minutes to wash the car; half an hour to clean the barbecue, an afternoon to sort out the bedrooms. Thinking in blocks of time helps us focus on what we can do in the time we have got available. We plan to set aside time if the job is going to take longer than we have got at the moment.

Children need help to see they can do this too. They need more help than they used to because life can be a lot more spontaneous now than it ever was in the past. You can decide to have a barbecue at six o'clock at night even if there is nothing in the house to eat. You can whizz down to the supermarket, pick up just what you need and you're off. The sausages will be sizzling by seven. Now that we use cars rather than buses, we aren't tied to timetables to get somewhere. We can simply decide to go and go. Planning what to watch on TV and when to watch it doesn't have to be so organised when there is more than one TV in the house. You can book holidays, do banking, and contact long-lost friends in the middle of the night if that is what you want to do. Because children don't see adults planning or hear them making detailed arrangements as much as they used to, parents need to draw attention to what planning means. Parents need to give their children opportunities to make plans, carry out plans, and check on whether those plans have worked. Children are interested in plans. Let them know what needs to be planned. Let them help with the planning. Let them learn how to plan.

Change it round

Your children will only change if you are making changes as well. They are behaving the way they are now because of the influences on them at the moment. To get them to change the way they are behaving, so that they will work with you, you will have to look at what you are doing and see how you can change it so that your children will get the opportunity to change.

Change the words

You might need to change the way you:

• Speak to them
• Ask them questions
• Praise them
• Criticise them

Lots of mothers have sons who they find take no notice of what they say. Oliver's mum would get irritated and feel hurt when Oliver would immediately do what his dad had asked him to do yet ignore it when she asked him to do anything. She felt rejected and it didn't matter how many treats she arranged for Oliver he still ignored her whenever she asked him to do anything.

Be straight

Oliver's mum had the same difficulty many women do. Women speak differently from men and hear things differently too. Usually if a man wants something done he will put it in the form of a command. Usually if a woman wants something done she will put it in the form of an invitation. Listen to yourself and try to spot how you ask someone to do something. Do you start with:

- Get the . . .
- Fetch the . . .
- Take . . .
- Go . . .
- Give . . . ?

Or do you start with:

- Would you . . .
- Could you . . .
- Can you . . .
- Shall we . . .
- Let's . . . ?

To many women, a command that starts with, 'Fetch the . . .' can sound rude, unfriendly and hostile. It is simply not the way they feel comfortable talking to others and they don't feel happy if people speak to them like that either. However if they try speaking like that to their sons they will probably find that boys who seemed unmotivated, lazy or unhelpful begin to do what they have been asked.

When some boys hear a command put in the form of an invitation, they think they are being asked whether they want to do it or not. They think it is optional and if they don't want to do it, feel they have been given a choice and it is OK for them to choose not to do it and in some cases not even to reply.

It is helpful to know that the way you speak to somebody influences the response you get. If you can be clear and brief when you speak to boys about what you want them to do, and conversational when you are having a discussion with them, then boys have a chance of being able to please you rather than feeling confused when you lose your temper.

Be clear if you want children to work with you

Communication is difficult whoever you are communicating with. Whenever you say something that doesn't get the response you were expecting, think about what you said or how you said it and see if there is some way you can adjust how you communicate so that other people will adjust how they communicate with you.

Don't blame yourself if things are going wrong. Communication is extremely difficult but worth trying to improve.

Change the time

Protect some time for the activities you think are important. If you think playing out is an important part of your children's day, make sure there is a time when they can do this. Don't just put it on your wish-list and then feel cheated or upset when it hasn't happened. If you think helping tidy up after dinner is important, don't agree to anything else happening until that tidying up is done. If you think your children should be in bed at nine o'clock, make sure they are getting ready for bed at half past eight. If you want them to remember to take everything they need to school, make sure there is protected time to get it ready. If you want to have proper conversations with them, protect time when that can happen.

If you don't protect time, then everyone can feel hurt and confused and nervous about what they are supposed to be doing, when they are supposed to be doing it, and how important they should make it.

There are always more things to do than there is time to do them.

You can help your child feel successful and keen to do more by helping them realise the importance of protecting time to do what has to be done.

Change the balance

Parents can feel that they need to be taking their children wherever they need to be. They can also feel that they should be sitting through practices or shopping while practices are happening. Parents can feel constantly driven by the pressures of paying attention to the needs of their children. It is important to keep a balance and a sense of proportion.

We all assume that the way we are spending our time is right although other people might despair at the way we are running round in circles or making extra work for ourselves. Every so often, try and hold on to a comment that a friend has made. At the time, their idea for how you could rearrange something may seem totally impossible. But if you keep that comment somewhere in your memory, you may see how you can change the 'unchangeable', do the 'undoable', or even think the 'unthinkable', so life is more agreeable.

Change the attention

Parents know the importance of paying attention to their children. Sometimes, that attention needs to be close attention where you are watching their every move ready to guide them at any moment. At other times, the attention can be arm's length attention where you are conscious of what they are doing but you don't need to interrupt what they are doing unless they go off track for some reason.

Motivation can be reduced if parents interfere too early or too late

When children are asked to set the table, they should be allowed to go as far as possible on the knowledge they have before there is any contribution from an adult. If the adult steps in too early making suggestions or giving instructions, the children will feel the adult is taking over. They may stay motivated to be an assistant or they may feel like giving up completely, but they will not be motivated to use their own knowledge.

If the adult steps in too late, the children can feel abandoned and vulnerable. They might make wild guesses about what they are supposed to do or stop altogether, because they can't see how or where to start. Adults need to be assessing and reassessing all the time what their input needs to be. This is a fascinating activity because helping someone develop confidence and skills is very creative. It is creative because how you respond to what the child is doing or what the needs of the activity are will affect the satisfaction that the children will feel and the motivation they will have to do that activity and other activities in the future. Children become demotivated when they believe that other people don't think that they can do something. What they haven't realised is that they have become demotivated because the adults involved didn't think about the impact of what they were doing.

Change the thinking

We can be under such pressure that we can start to feel it would be easier if we could all function as robots. Then we could just get on with what needs to be done. If we could be focused, concentrate, have commitment, have endless supplies of energy and drive, then all our ambitions could be met. But we are not robots. We are people who are creative, thoughtful, uncertain and fragile.

We can meet our ambitions if we can:

• Find outlets for our creativity
• Have time to think
• Know that our thinking can be extraordinarily imaginative
• Know that our thinking can be completely focused when it needs to be

Finding a balance

Finding a balance between the desire to be free of all restraints and to explore all the possibilities, yet still be able to put to one side those imaginings in order to tune in to the demands of the moment, is the secret of motivation. Too much of one or the other will destroy motivation. The truly motivated person can change the balance from moment to moment.

What if

People who think 'What if . . .' but can also think, 'Not now . . .' will be able to energise themselves and the people around them. The person who simply thinks 'What if . . .' is exhausting to be with because they have either never realised they are responsible for any part of their life or they have abandoned that responsibility. The person who never thinks 'What if . . .' is also exhausting to be with, because they have no creative energy to get going.

Whenever children create a situation where they are going round in circles or flying off out of your reach, they will need you to step in to remind them to check exactly what they have to do. They need to check back to make sure they are bearing in mind all the instructions they have been given and not just the aspect of it that has caught their imagination.

I do what I love

Harry's homework was to find some everyday object around the home and then imagine that an archaeologist was digging it up in a thousand years' time. He had to describe it the way the archaeologist would, so he wasn't to say what it was used for or what it was called, he was only to describe the detail of it. By the end of his description, anyone in his class should be able to have an informed guess as to its name.

The second part of his homework, if there was time, was to draw the object on a piece of card and then cut it up into pieces that could be fitted back together like a jigsaw. The aim was that nobody would be able to tell by looking at just one piece of the jigsaw what the whole thing was. The object would only become obvious once the jigsaw pieces were fitted together.

Harry was thrilled with the idea of the jigsaw. He loved craft activities. He searched the house for a suitable piece of cardboard. He was going to do a jigsaw of a telephone. The suggestion at the bottom of the homework sheet was that the children could use the card from a cereal packet. Much reorganisation went on as Harry tipped the bird seed from its plastic container into a bag, washed and dried the plastic container and then upended the cereal packet into the plastic box so that he could have the cardboard. Time was running out.

Harry was completely motivated to find the cardboard. He was completely motivated to do the jigsaw and in a complete fog about the written description. His parents were happy that he was busy getting on with his homework and hadn't checked exactly what the homework was. When they realised he had left out the written description, they knew they would have to give him a 100 per cent support. They knew that Harry wouldn't be able to open his mind to creating a description in words. They wanted Harry to take in his homework on time so they teamed up with Harry to get it done.

Make sure it's teamwork

When you are teaming up with your child to help them to get something done, remember that any idea that takes you towards the goal is all right. In Harry's example he couldn't think how he could describe the telephone he had chosen. His mum and dad made some suggestions. As they made them they jotted them down for Harry on a scrap of paper. They realised there was no point in getting Harry to write them down. Harry's parents responded really well because they wrote down what they said so that Harry could choose what he wanted to use and how he wanted to use it. Quite often when several people are doing something together there is enough flexibility on the way to getting it done to let everyone have an input. It is important for everyone to know that they are part of a team. Each member makes a contribution and someone else carries it a step further.

Maybe you need to give 100 per cent support

Whenever children are at a full stop they are going to need your support. It might need to be a 100 per cent of your support. When you are giving a 100 per cent of your support, it means you are close enough to watch and to monitor everything your children are doing:

- You will be thinking about what support you need to offer next
- You might need to suggest the next idea or solve the next problem
- You might need to suggest a sentence or make sure the layout is right
- Wherever you see the children coming off the track you will be ready to step in with the help they need to make sure they are getting something out of what they are doing. They will be gaining confidence that what they are doing is heading in the right direction
- Children will be beginning to trust their ideas
- They will be starting to see how they can build on their knowledge with their ideas
- They will be beginning to see that there is a sequence to what they are doing and there is a way of reaching the standard that has been set
- They will be realising that they can work with you

11

Organisational skills
for children

When there is no organisation

I've said it a hundred times and so ...
I can't understand why:

* He always leaves something behind
* He doesn't hand in homework that he has done and is in his bag
* She doesn't bother to untie her laces and spends ages trying to drag the shoes off when it would be much faster if she undid them first
* She keeps on writing with a blunt pencil when there is a sharp one in her pencil case

In the long run
Children have very little idea of the long run because they have only lived a short time. They don't know what they can get away with and what will keep coming back to haunt them. Adults know these things because they have had plenty of chances to find out that some things, even if they are trivial, are better sorted out immediately.

Just do the best you can

Sometimes you see small children whose shorts or trousers don't fit properly. They are just a little bit too large. All day they have to keep hoisting them up. They don't let their droopy drawers stop them doing what they want to do, they just try and manage as best they can.

As adults, we probably wouldn't leave the house until we had found a belt or a different pair of trousers. We wouldn't be able to bear the idea of having to worry about what was slipping all day. Whenever children have to cope with something such as their clothes not fitting, they may get the idea that it is OK to just do the best you can.

Just get on

A child may know that having a sharp pencil gives the best result. One day there are no sharp pencils for them to use, and when they tell the teacher, she says they should just get on with the one they have got because there isn't time to get some sharpened now. The child gets on with the blunt pencil and remembers that the next time they have a blunt pencil the teacher may not want to know.

Just hurry up

In the same way, this could happen with shoes. Someone who can't see the child taking their shoes off is shouting at them to hurry up. The child tries to undo his laces, but they become knotted. In his panic to be quick, the child yanks off his shoes, leaving a frustratingly tight knot in the laces. The child has, at least, stopped the person shouting and got his shoes off.

In each of these cases the child has solved the problem in the short term. The children only have a short-term view of the world because they have no power to have a long-term view.

To take a long-term view, children would have to have power over the clothes they are given, control over the sharpening of pencils, and an ability to explain that they need a little more time to take their shoes off. They would have to have power over time, priorities and outcomes.

These examples show how children can learn to have a short-term view of the things they are responsible for. There is nothing wrong with a short-term view in its place. A long-term view needs to be taught, however. Children need to learn how to think ahead and how to plan.

The stages in learning the long-term view
- At any age there will be things which we can't control, but the older we get the more things we can organise
- As we get older, we will have had plenty of chances to see the benefit of organising ahead
- As we get older, we will also have had plenty of chances to see and learn from other people's experiences
- As we get older, we will have plenty of chances to see the problems that can happen if we don't plan ahead

Watch and learn
Adults often pass on information to their friends, neighbours, relations and acquaintances. They pass on information in the hopes that it will help others avoid the mistakes they have made. They pass on information in the hopes that others will benefit from what they have found out. They often take up recommendations from other people about where to go on holiday, which are good restaurants, the best route to get somewhere, or the cheapest place to find something.

How children can learn from other people's experiences
Stories, whether on film, tape or video, whether in books or comics, are great ways for children to find out what happens when people behave in different ways. These are safe ways to explore the wider world. Children can identify with the characters, go where they go, and see what they see, without having to be responsible for the consequences of what the characters do or don't do.

Everyone else knows so . . .

I can't understand why:

- He doesn't know his teacher's name
- She doesn't know where her parents work or what they do
- She doesn't know what her telephone number is
- He doesn't know where we are going this afternoon

The framework

There are many things that children won't necessarily be asked about but which people would expect them to know. These pieces of information are part of the child's framework.

Having a framework provides children with certainty, security and sense. They have the certainty that their family members have an existence even when they can't see them; they have a security that the separate existences of the people in their family don't mean that family members are lost to each other when they are out of sight; they have a sense that everyone has a wider world than they can see and a wider world than they are part of.

How do children build a framework?

- They can be encouraged to learn key facts – address, telephone number, how many grandparents they have, what their parents do, how many aunts and uncles they have, and where their brothers and sisters go to school.
- They can be encouraged to ask you questions in the same way that you ask them questions – What did you do today? Who did you see today? What did you have for lunch today? And did you have a nice day? When you tell them what you did, you give them an idea of what sort of thing they could tell you about.

Check whether your children know all the things you think they should know. You may be surprised to discover that many children, even in their teens, have not started to build a framework that involves knowledge of their family and their locality.

A framework is a springboard to the wider world.

Noting and noticing

Motivated children are noticing things all the time. They notice that they are awake; they notice that they are up and ready for action; they notice what they will need to do next, and they notice if they have time to fit something else in.

How do they notice?
They notice:

- By being told something directly
- By overhearing other people talking
- By hearing other people asking questions and listening to the answers they get
- By having other people interested in the fact they have noticed
- By having other people interested in the facts they have noticed
- By looking around

What is wrong with them?
I can't understand why:

- He doesn't just do what he is supposed to
- She doesn't get on with it when it's really easy

Holding out for a better offer

Children who don't get on with something that could be done are often holding out for a better offer. They feel certain that someone else will do it for them because they have wasted so much time. They feel they can avoid doing it altogether because no one else has the time to sort it out. The danger for these children is that they are so clever at avoiding doing what they should be doing that no one has the time or the energy to motivate them to get on.

Breaking the habit

You can't change the whole situation in one go. You have to see it in the same light as breaking a habit.

To break a habit:

- You need to close off the options
- Choose something you want your child to do that he usually puts off in the hope it will be forgotten
- Make sure you won't forget what it is. The best thing to do is choose something small, such as putting out the rubbish

Short and sweet

Step One – Say when the job has to be done by. You don't want to have to keep checking whether it has been done, all you want to know is that it has been done.

Step Two – Make the instruction very straightforward: 'Collect up the rubbish from the kitchen and all the bins around the house. Put all the rubbish in the bin outside and then on Tuesday morning take the big bin to the road. Bring the big bin back when it has been emptied.'

Step Three – Congratulate the child if it has been done well. Find out if there were any difficulties. Make any suggestions which you think would be helpful for next time.

Step Four – If the job isn't being done well, do it once or twice yourself, to find where the problems might be. You need to check that what you thought was straightforward really *is* straightforward.

Checking beats disappointment

If you are doing something new, you need to check that it can be done the way you are planning to do it. When you have done something before you know where the hidden difficulties are. When you are doing something for the first time, you can commit yourself to time or money that will be wasted if you haven't given yourself a chance to check each step. We all know that details we could have checked but have left unchecked go on to cause us many more problems in the long run.

Trial runs
- Prevent errors in the end
- Give you thinking time
- Allow you to adjust your pace
- Open up options
- Give you the chance to check

Have a trial run before you go all the way. Trial runs are motivating in the long run.

Homework

It is always better to do homework on scrap paper first. It doesn't all need to be done in rough, but it is important to make sure that children are on the right track. If they don't have a go in rough first but do their homework straight into their book, they don't have a chance to sort out any problems.

When they realise that they could have done the homework much better, they have to decide whether to rip out the pages and start again or hand in work which they know could have been improved. They will feel fed up because they know that their teacher will either think that this is the best that they can do or that they can't be bothered. They will feel annoyed because they have let themselves down, and feel frustrated because they haven't given themselves the chance to show what they really can do.

Scrap paper means just that; sheets of paper that you can use to try out ideas on. Collect junk mail that has only been printed on one side, the unused pages in old exercise books and large, used envelopes.

What's holding Ali back?

Ali didn't like doing homework and this was reflected in the marks he got. It was a pity because his end of year exam results were usually quite good, but whenever teachers talked about moving him up to the next set, someone always remembered his very poor homework, so Ali always stayed where he was.

The reason that Ali's homework was always poor was that he flung himself at the homework, anxious to get it done, and in his rush to get it finished he would miss out questions, misread instructions and muddle up his ideas. On top of this, because he never thought beforehand how he was going to present the work, it would look messy, confused and difficult to follow.

Make a space to sort out the pace

To improve the marks he got for his homework, Ali needed to get into the habit of changing his pace to fit the homework task. Successful people know how to operate using a variety of paces even within the same task. They also know the importance of slowing the pace down so that they give themselves a chance to be completely prepared at each step.

Doing homework in rough would give Ali:

- The space to sort out the pace
- The chance to change the pace that had worked for the thing he had been doing before he started his homework
- The chance to ignore the pace of the thing he wanted to do after he had finished his homework
- The opportunity to focus on what needed to be done
- The chance to develop a pace for doing his homework which was appropriate for getting the work done

What he had been doing was giving no special pace to the homework. He had been trying to do it at the pace of what else was going on, whether that was the football match he had just been in or the conversation he had been having with his mates.

Find out what is wanted

To improve the marks he got for his homework enough to be able to move up to the next set, Ali needed a checklist against which he knew his work was being measured. Ali's parents tried to help him by making a list of key points which teachers look for in homework. When they went to Parents' Night, they checked with the teacher that if Ali addressed these key points in his homework his marks would improve. The teacher agreed and added a few of his own criteria. The list included things such as underlining the title and the date, answering all the questions that had been set, using capital letters and showing that what had been covered in the lesson had been understood.

We all need to be clear about what we need to do in order to do it well and not to lose marks for it. The criteria for doing well are not optional if you want to do well. There is a discipline to be learned if you want to be working with the best. Part of that discipline is that you aim for full marks. You recognise that every time you settle for less you are actually losing a mark. Not underlining the title and the date can mean losing a mark and also may lose you credibility with your teacher. Being credible means you are making the effort to maximise your opportunities. Being credible does not mean being better than everyone else, but being the best you can be at any moment.

Ali grew up

Ali overcame his dislike of doing homework and chose to sort out capital letters as the first thing he could do to improve his homework. He worked out that if he did the work in rough first he had a better chance of spotting mistakes and putting them right before copying it up in ink.

The organised way to make a poster

Emily came home from school with an A3 piece of blue card. Everyone in the class had been given a piece of card and been told to design a poster to advertise the school fair that was being held later in the month. They had been told the information that must appear on the poster; the date; the time; the place and the entrance fee. Emily was very excited. She loved drawing and designing and she was good at it.

Working it out

The first thing Emily did was to get a piece of newspaper that was the same size as the poster. Because Emily wasn't used to drawing on such a large piece of paper she wanted to make sure she got her proportions right and had enough space to fit on all the information as well as her illustrations and border.

Emily practised on a piece of scrap paper each detail that she wanted to have on the final poster. She experimented with types of lettering and her different pens. When she was happy that she knew what she was doing she got together everything she needed, found a space big enough to spread out her work, and got started on the actual poster.

Emily knew the value of organising the space in her time, the place she would work, and the pace she would work at.

Get it better every time

Peter was highly motivated. He really wanted to improve his GCSE mark in his resit because he knew the job he wanted and he needed a good grade in English to get it. He was prepared to do his work on scrap paper first and was happy to have it checked before rewriting it.

Learn by your mistakes

However, when he did copy his work out in best, it would still have all the mistakes that had been there in the rough version. It seemed there was another skill that Peter had to learn.

He had to learn to let go of his first ideas of what was right. He had to learn how to clear his mind so that when he looked at the rough draft he could actually see the corrections that had been made and he could think about them and incorporate them into his final draft.

- He needed to know that he could look around to see what other people were doing so he could work out what he could do and therefore not cause anyone distress
- He needed to know how he could do something to reassure his teacher that he was back on track once he had upset his teacher (or anyone else)

What Huw's parents needed to know
- That Huw had picked up his way of behaving with other people by watching them
- That the damage this had done didn't have to be long-term
- That they could find ways to be models for Huw that would help him get on better with other children

What Huw needed to try
- To find a place to sit or stand so he wasn't alarming people by moving around all the time
- To let himself be a passive member of a group by being interested, but not saying or doing anything unless asked. His activity could be mental activity. He could watch the situation as if he were a reporter or a writer who might at some point write down or draw or record everything he had noticed. If that was too difficult, Huw could count to a hundred slowly to himself, or recite nursery rhymes to himself, to help him remember that he was trying to be part of the group, but in a way that the rest of the group could be at peace
- To learn ways of starting a conversation where people would feel friendly towards him

Children who learn these techniques can quickly become part of the group. They have been given a strategy which they can soon use. They know a way to make sure they will sit still so they can pay attention to what else is going on. If they start to go off the rails they know a way to calm themselves down and be still.

Huw was empowered

What Huw tried was enough to give him space to build up the confidence in others to be able to trust him. His social skills developed as he tried out ways of making friends.

Motivate your child to be his own person

Motivation and emotion

We are often put off our stride by a comment that someone else makes. The comment may have been made as a deliberate attack or it may have been a careless remark. How we handle comments that upset us or cause us to think about whether the comment was reasonable will influence how we are motivated in the future.

Families have lots of stories about how a chance remark stopped someone else doing something which they had loved doing before.

Dancing is sad

Charlotte came home from school saying she didn't want to go to the dancing lessons, which she had pleaded to be allowed to go to, any more. Someone at school had told her that dancing was for 'sad' people.

German is for losers

Freddie arrived home and announced that he wasn't going to choose German when it came to the time to pick the subjects he would be sitting at GCSE. This was a shock, as Freddie had always done really well at German, and at Parents' Evening the teacher had said what great hopes she had for how well Freddie would do in the subject. Freddie said that his best friend wasn't going to choose German and had said the reason he wasn't going to do it was that it was a waste of time. English was the most important language and German was for 'losers'.

Hamsters are pathetic

Kylie got a hamster for Christmas. She loved it. It was a very important part of her life. She played with it after school and was very good about cleaning its cage out.

One day Kylie arrived home from school looking ashen. She didn't get her hamster out. This was extraordinary. After a while she started to cry. There had been a conversation at playtime when her group of friends had been saying what a stupid pet a hamster was. They hadn't seemed to remember that she had a hamster and she hadn't reminded them as they all joked and laughed about what a pathetic pet it was and how hamsters never really did anything apart from eat, sleep and run round on a wheel.

It's not what you say, it's the way that I hear it

There are some things which are said without malice or which are said without meaning to undermine people's self-belief. It is the way that it is heard that does the damage. In Kylie's case, just hearing the conversation made her doubt herself. She wasn't sure whether what she loved was worth loving and how she would ever know what was worth loving.

If children can weigh up what they hear, acknowledge the truth or untruth in the statement but still feel motivated to carry on, a malicious remark will have no effect on an individual's belief in himself or herself. Not everyone lets themselves be affected by comments which are malicious, or which could damage reputations or friendship groups.

What to do when something goes wrong in your child's social world

Children's motivation can easily be affected by something going wrong in their social world.

If children learn to value who they are, what they can do and what motivates them, they will be protected against the '. . . slings and arrows of outrageous fortune . . .' that come their way.

Bullying

Simon was being bullied at school. He was a pleasant boy and had always been able to make friends. His parents noticed something was wrong when his marks began to go down but he couldn't tell them what the problem was. He began to look pale and lost his appetite. Finally, he told his parents that there was a boy at school who was not in his class but who seemed to delight in small acts of nastiness. He 'bumped' into Simon in the corridor but always made it look accidental. If he was ahead when Simon was going through a door he would let the door go rather than hold it back. He always muttered Simon's name as he walked by in a sort of menacing way.

Simon's parents were in a dilemma:

- Would the school take any information seriously? They might think that everything this bully did was trivial even though the effect on Simon wasn't trivial at all
- They tried suggesting that Simon ignored him but Simon couldn't seem to do this

The problem with telling someone to ignore bullying is that you leave them in a vacuum. If a child is at a loss to know what to do when they are feeling bullied it is better to give them something to do when the bullying is happening.

The danger of telling someone to stand up to a bully is that they may not feel able to do so. They may not be the type of person who can cope with a confrontation.

If an adult gives a child a definite instruction that the child is really unable to follow, the child can end up feeling more wretched than he did before. He couldn't cope with the bullying and now he can't cope with what he is being told to do about the bullying.

Honour what children can do. Support them while they try and work out what will work for them. Often by the time they have worked it out the problem has stopped.

Tell them what you do

Think of what you do at the dentist. How do you take your mind off what the dentist is doing? Your child needs similar techniques for coping with a bully. Something to occupy his mind and dilute the effect of the bully. One successful suggestion might be to sing a favourite song. Singing it to themselves gives them power. Another suggestion is for your child to imagine himself as full of light, laughter or strength.

When a bully is successful, he has made his victim feel full of self-doubt. He has defined his victim. Victims need help to re-define themselves.

Suggestions that help your child feel more confident will dispel the doubt and replace it with self-belief.

Bitchiness

Sharda had just started at secondary school. She had been really looking forward to it. She started with her friend who was the only other person from her primary school going to that school. Sharda had been looking forward to being at the bigger school with all the opportunities for meeting new people and the lovely sports facilities that were there. All through the holidays she just couldn't wait for the start of term to arrive. She couldn't get there quickly enough. But after three weeks of the new school year she was crying every night. She couldn't cope with being in a big school. At her old school everybody was very friendly and kind. They all knew each other and each other's families.

Now she felt alone and frightened when she heard the sort of comments which some of the girls made about the other girls. She was terrified that one day they might be made about her.

Sharda's friend seemed to have really settled in to school. She was keen on all the acting that happened there, and she had joined a couple of drama clubs already. Sharda was not interested in drama at all and felt that she had lost her only ally. No one was being nasty to her in particular, but she was just not used to the bitchiness that she kept hearing. She started to say that she didn't want to go to school.

Think nice thoughts

When people – children or adults – make bitchy comments, it always says more about them than it does about the person who is being commented on. Many of us have friends who make unpleasant comments but we have learned to hear the comments yet not let them interfere with the friendship. Share with your children what you do when someone makes bitchy comments to you.

Do You:

- Think to yourself something positive about the person who is being criticised?
- Think to yourself something positive about the person who is making the remark?
- Rather than responding, introduce a different topic?
- Be quiet and let the conversation pass?

The 'in crowd'

Wesley had always been interested in sports, Scouts and family life. His family had always done things together but suddenly he wanted to give it all up because at his school it was not cool to belong to youth groups or sports clubs. The cool thing for the pupils at his school was hanging round the shopping centre and sitting on benches on the main street. He began pestering his parents to let him give up all his activities because he said otherwise his life was going to be a misery at school. Whenever they tried to suggest that there were other people in his year who were different from the 'in crowd' he said that they were not important, they were not who he wanted to be with. Wesley was listening to the 'in crowd' and thought that what they were saying and doing was right. He felt as if what he was doing was old-fashioned and childish.

Give them some options

In the face of the onslaught of the 'in crowd' give your child the chance to find some other activity which he finds cool but which has the level of supervision that you are happy with. You will be showing your child that you recognise he is growing up and his needs and interests are changing. You are also showing him that you respect his need to choose something himself, but that you expect him to find something which will keep him safe and keep you from feeling worried.

Being an outsider

Rachel had moved with her family to a new area where they stood out like a sore thumb. Their accents were different and they hadn't yet worked out how to fit into this community. They loved it in their new home and all the families they had met had been really friendly but at school Rachel felt it was different. Everyone poked fun at the way she talked and they laughed at her ideas about anything. Her parents tried inviting other children from school back for tea and although that seemed to go really well Rachel told them it made no difference when they got in to school the next day. It was as if the night before hadn't happened.

Give it time

Being laughed at is a horrible feeling and you can think the situation will never change but it often does. Some people just need to get used to seeing a new face around. It is not unusual for people to only notice the things that are different when they meet someone new. After a few months they forget about the newness and enjoy the new friend.

The 'swot'

When Michaela's mum went to Parents' Evening, the teacher told her that her daughter was becoming quiet in class. Michaela had always loved school and had always done very well in school. She was a natural scholar who enjoyed the challenges which teachers set her, and she had been enthusiastic about everything that went on at school. Now, in the last year at primary school, the teacher felt there must be something troubling her.

Michaela's parents felt, after having talked to their daughter, that she was worrying about how hard she was working and how well she was doing.

There were other children who were bright in her class but Michaela had always come top. Michaela said that the other children had started to call her a brain-box and kept coming to her to ask for the answers to the homework questions. It seemed that their daughter was trying to hold herself back and hide her ability so that she wouldn't get noticed.

Michaela's parents were really worried that what she was doing might affect the reports about her ability when she went to secondary school. They knew that she was capable of being at the top and would want to be doing her best. They felt Michaela was being caught in two ways: First, she didn't want the other children to keep asking her questions because she felt intimidated, and sometimes ridiculed, when they did so. Second, she didn't want to limit what she could do at school because she had always found it so exciting taking up challenges.

Where do you want to be?
When children are made to feel that they should feel ashamed at, or embarrassed by, being good at something, it is helpful to get them to think about:

• Other people who enjoy being good at some activity
• Where they want to be in four years' time when they probably won't see the people who are giving them a hard time now
• What sort of a person do they want to be? Do they want to be what someone else tells them they should be or do they want to be the person they know they are or the person they know they can be?

The 'eccentric'
Jack loved to put on his video of Riverdance and leap around. He wanted to be a dancer as soon as he could find a group to join. He loved to practise steps that he had learned from the video. He told

everyone that his ankles and his feet just kept moving and they were full of the rhythm. He was an enthusiast about life and loved to share his enthusiasms. Other children found him strange. They were not at all sure how to handle him and they were worried that they would be laughed at if they played with him. Jack did not seem to notice that other children found him a bit odd but his parents worried that as he got older he would stop being who he was and would start to worry about what others thought about him.

You can be who you are
Children who like things that are different to other children need to be helped to understand that they can be who they are and follow their own enthusiasms as long as they let other people be and do what *they* want. There are things which make you 'you' and children with great passion often turn into adults who get great pleasure from their enthusiasms.

The child who stammered
Edward stammered and the stammer got worse if he felt nervous. All the children in his class understood about his stammering and gave him time to say what he wanted. He joined a club that some of his friends from school went to. It was an activities club where they went roller-skating, kite flying, go-karting etc. He loved the club but one of the leaders didn't understand that Edward could cope. He kept speaking for him. Edward's parents didn't want to stop him going to the club but they didn't want him to lose the strength he had. They were worried that their son would stop speaking for himself and think that someone else would speak for him all the time. They were worried that their son would lose the motivation to communicate for himself.

Make your own chances
It is important that we all realise that it is up to us to take charge of our own lives. Sometimes this may mean that we rely on other people because we know we need help. Other times we will be

independent, push our own boundaries, be daring, take a risk. The most independent people know that either option is fine and it is up to them to choose.

When your children need support you could:

- Role-play with your children how to step in politely if someone is trying to talk over the top of their heads
- Borrow a book from the library and see how other people with the same problem cope
- Teach them to maintain eye-contact rather than look away when they are trying to say something – the other person will know that the communication is still going on, even if at that moment nothing is being said

The shy child

Preeya was very shy. She never spoke at school but she loved to be on the edge of a group watching what was going on. At home she was very chatty but the minute she was with anyone outside the family she was very quiet. People reacted in two ways. They either let Preeya go at her own pace or they made lots of suggestions to try and motivate her to feel that she could be included and other people would help her find a way to be included.

Get in control

To help a child who is very shy you can:

- Insist that they always say hello and goodbye to people.
- Get them to practise speaking loudly. To start with, give them a sentence and then have them whisper it back to you like a breath of wind, then squeak it like a mouse and then say it like a cat, bark it like a dog and roar it like a lion. This helps them realise that they have to do different things with their breath to get out different sounds. To do this means they need to change the amount of air they are taking in and how they control that air coming out. They realise that they have a choice about how

loudly or quietly they say something. Many children who speak quietly will have thought that they only have one volume. When they realise how to use their breath then they will know that they have an in-built volume control.

- Help them to realise that other people are shy. They may not notice that someone else is shy because that person appears to be so confident.
- Help them realise that overcoming shyness is like learning to walk. When you learn to walk you learn how to control your body. This means that you can go anywhere. When you learn to control your shyness you learn how to control your emotions. This means that you can go anywhere as well.

How you can motivate a child to share

Some children feel that if they share they are losing something quite vital. You can hear the tension in their voice whenever a sharing situation is in progress. Any game that means they have to share pieces becomes a battleground where they are either the aggressor or the victim. They can't see themselves as equal.

If you are helping someone to cope with sharing remember that it will take time and patience.

Ten tips to help children see that sharing is sensible

1. Compliment them every time they do something that looks like sharing so they build up a view of themselves as a 'sharing kind of person'.
2. Stop them playing the game if they refuse to share.
3. Have meals where the food is in the middle of the table and people take a share of that food.
4. Avoid giving them things that are just for them.
5. Help them see that they can share your time or your gifts and this doesn't take away anything from them.
6. If you are going to visit a friend make sure your child is taking something that can be shared. It might be something

to eat, something to play with or something to watch or listen to.

7. Children start to see the morality of sharing if they go and feed ducks at the pond. Children who hate sharing can feel quite outraged when one duck wants to take more than the others and so the others miss out.

8. Have conversations where you are interested in the people that your child knows. Don't only ask, 'Did you have a nice time?', but ask how things were for other people too.

9. Share jobs as well as treats.

10. Share choices of where to go and what to do.

How you can motivate a child to be friendly

Some children appear to be unfriendly because they haven't realised that other people are noticing them. They feel shy, unimportant, or as if they are the only one who should be noticed. It takes quite a lot of support to help children feel comfortable with the people around them. Some children are born friendly but most children need some help.

Ten tips for making friends

1. Encourage the children to think about other people. Talk to children about the other people in their lives so that they become more than just a face. Talk about what another person does, where they live, what they enjoy.

2. Insist that your child says hello and goodbye to people they have been with.

3. It is friendly to take care of someone else's possessions, so teach the child how to do that. It is very unfriendly to kick someone's ball into the pond or rip a page in someone else's book.

4. It is friendly to ask somebody about themselves.

5. It is friendly to offer to help.

6. It is friendly to reassure people when they feel worried.

7. Teach your child to stand up straight and look at people's faces.

8. Teach your child that it is friendly to volunteer.

9. Teach your child that it is friendly to play a game with other people so that everyone can have fun. You don't play to win when you are having a fun game, you play so that everyone can have a turn.
10. Practise smiling because it is friendly to smile.

How you can motivate a child to be polite

When politeness is missing we can feel:

- Uncertain
- Frightened
- Demotivated
- Unsupported
- At sea

Children need to know that if they are polite to other people they make them feel confident, safe, motivated, supported and affirmed. Politeness is not just about saying the words you have been taught but also knowing that when you are polite to people you are showing your respect towards them and showing self-respect as well.

Encouraging children to be polite is time well spent.

Ten tips for encouraging children to be polite
1. Insist on 'please' and 'thank you' especially to family members.
2. Insist your children understand other children have feelings as well.
3. Help your children realise that adults have feelings that can be affected by the way children behave. It is all right to tell your children when you are unhappy. It is essential to tell them when you are happy. Children love to be involved in conversations about the reasons adults have for the way they feel.
4. Make sure you have a list of 'feeling' words somewhere on a wall or fridge. Use the words when you have chats with your children about what they have been doing, where they have

been, and who they have been with. You will find your children have lots to tell you if you give them the chance.

5. Make sure your children understand that they need to speak loudly enough for the other person to hear.
6. Try out ways of chatting to adults.
7. Practise ways of asking for something, particularly when you are visiting friends and relations. It is possible to remind an adult of a nice experience you have had with them in the past without asking directly for the treat again. In that way the adult can engage in a conversation about the shared memory without feeling pressurised to provide that treat again.
8. Expect to tidy up if you have helped make a mess. It is sometimes important to ask what you can help with and how you can help before you start.
9. Expect to say hello and goodbye whenever you are with people.
10. Teach your children to introduce their friends to you and to any other people who may be in the group.

How you can motivate a child to be considerate

When people are considerate to others they are thinking of the needs of someone else.

Ten tips to make sure you are invited again

1. Other people's time matters. Try to make sure you let people know if you are going to be late. Let people know if your plans with them have changed. Your children need to know that you expect them to let you know if they are changing their plans. Let your children know that you have to let other people know when you are changing your plans.
2. Teach your children to use the phone so they can ring and let people know if plans are changing. Part of that call is to check whether the change of plan will fit in with other people's arrangements.
3. Children need to know that they are responsible for the marks their hands and shoes make. Teach them to check whether

their hands and nails are clean. Teach them to check whether their shoes are dirty. Children should learn that they can offer to take their shoes off whenever they visit someone else's house, especially if their shoes are dirty.

4. Teach your children to become aware when they have to wait. There are many times when they will need to wait. They will learn from you how to do it. If they see you becoming angry and impatient, they will assume that is how everybody in your family should wait. They need to learn that everybody has to wait sometimes. They are not being victimised when they wait. They can think about ways of shortening the wait or making the wait interesting. They can learn to notice what is around so they don't need to get bored even if there is quite a long wait. They need to learn to wait for their turn, wait for someone else to catch up, wait for you to speak to somebody, wait to cross a road and wait in a queue.

5. When children write thank-you letters, they show people who have given them a gift or done something special for them that they appreciate the effort or the thought.

6. When children put back toys, equipment or anything else they have used or borrowed and they leave equipment in a state where the next person can get started straight away, they show they consider other people to be as important as themselves. They take responsibility for the next person feeling valued. They take responsibility for the fact that the next person will feel unhappy, devalued or inconvenienced if things are not the way they should be. Motivation stays high when people feel that their needs have been considered.

7. Children need practise to work out the level of noise that is fair to other people. They need to learn that sometimes they have to be silent, sometimes they can have a quiet conversation, sometimes they can call out or speak up and that sometimes they can be raucous.

8. Do not let your children feel that any time they want something you will stop everything and get it for them. You do not have to answer them every time they speak to you. They need

to work out whether the time is right to interrupt. If they pick up the idea that they can interrupt any time and anywhere when they are with you, then they will believe they can interrupt wherever they are and with whomever they are. They will cause havoc.

9. Teach your children to close doors quietly, to sit down, not bounce down, to keep feet under control, and to use messy equipment in a place that will not cause damage.

10 Considerate people know that everything they do has consequences. They can have a pleasant impact on other people or they can lessen the impact of something unpleasant if they are considerate.

How you can motivate a child to take turns

Some children seem happy to take turns from a very early age. Other children need help to see why they have to take turns. Children who cannot take turns are children who don't understand. If your children will not take turns it will be because they have not understood why taking turns works.

Taking turns works because:

- It gives a structure
- It shares out something between more than one person
- It protects everyone's right to have a go or have some, no matter how small, weak or inexpert they are
- It is more fun

Ten tips to teach turn-taking

1. Play with children so you can act as umpire.
2. Whenever a child is not taking turns, remove what is not being shared and hand it to another person in the game or group.
3. Point out that people will not want to play with them if they do not take turns.
4. Have a time limit on the turn so the children know that the length of the turn is limited.

5. Take opportunities for turn-taking – turns to switch lights on or off, to sit in a favourite seat in the car, to answer the phone, to sit on the most comfortable chair, to choose the meal, to have first bath or to open the door.

6. If you have an only child, share turn-taking with them so they get used to the idea.

7. Turn-taking needs to be seen as positive no matter whose turn it is. Help your child enjoy watching another person having a turn. Some children think that nothing is happening that they need to be interested in, if it is not their turn.

8. If your child thinks that the turn-taking is never fair to them they can make a chart recording the turn they had and how long it lasted and the turn other people had and how long their turns lasted.

9. If your child gets upset because it always seems to be somebody else's birthday and not theirs, get them to make a chart of all the months of the year for each family member. They can colour in each month as it passes. This will show them that it is the calendar that decides who will have the next birthday. The earth goes round the sun once a year and when it gets to the place it was when they were born that will be their birthday.

10. If your child gets upset because someone else in the family seems to get chances that they can never have and so they will never get the chance to have a turn in the same way, explain that some things are just a matter of time and place. You and they can keep an eye out for the thing that is going to be at the right time and the right place for them.

How you can motivate a child to cope with losing

You have to try to do your best always, but your best may not mean you win. People who become winners learn how to cope with the disappointment of missing the trophy. They know there will always be another day or that it is time to move on. No one wants to lose, but if they do lose they need to learn how to lose well.

Checklist for losing

1. Did I do my best?
2. How do I know I did my best?
3. Will there be a next time?
4. Was there something I could have done differently?
5. What will I do differently next time?
6. Did I learn something I can use next time?
7. Is there another thing I could do that I would be better at?
8. Should I make a big change or a small change?
9. Do I have to win to have satisfaction?
10. What is the worst thing that can happen because I didn't win?

How you can motivate a child to eat what is on the plate

When you believe your child should eat what you have put out for him to eat, you will have no trouble managing it.

Ten tips for making eating enjoyable

1. Put a very small amount of the food your child resists on the plate.
2. Stand your ground – this is easier if you have made the portion small and you are not trying to argue about them eating a lot.
3. Once your child has eaten a small bit at one meal, you can ask whether he is grown up enough to take a slightly larger amount at the next meal. Children love to feel that what they are doing is making them grow up.
4. Involve the child in the preparation – taking the food from the fridge, putting the food into dishes or plates for the table, or chopping up vegetables.
5. Eat with them. You establish a time for eating. They have a chance to see you relishing your food. Make sure they ask before they leave the table. Create a ritual that will support what you are trying to do.
6. Rank different foods. Ask them what is their favourite food,

their next favourite food and so on. Food becomes something you can chat about rather than get hostile over.

7. Try to put questions about food positively. Make your own comments positive as well.
8. Make up lists of words you can use to describe food – taste, texture, ingredients and the way it is cooked.
9. Have little tasting sessions where there are several old favourites, one they think they don't like and a couple of new tastes.
10. Include food as part of the enjoyment. Take food for a picnic. The important part of the outing is the walk. You will take a picnic but that is at the end. The child will be hungry and relaxed. There is something about a picnic that makes us all feel more open to new experiences and ideas.

How you can motivate a child to get up in the morning

For many families, early morning is a fraught time – especially if children need to be up and ready by a particular time.

Ten tips for making mornings manageable

1. Encourage children to work out how long they need in the morning to do all the things they want to do.
2. Encourage them to work out how long they need to be up in the morning to do all the things they need to do.
3. Get them to work out a sensible 'go to bed' time so they have had enough sleep to be able to get going in the morning.
4. If they have difficulty getting to sleep and/or are very hot in bed, and then have trouble waking up, see if a different diet before bed will help them have a better sleep.
5. Experiment with morning routines to see which one means they can sort out what they want to do and need to do.
6. Experiment with how far the curtains are open. How wide open should the window be?
7. Suggest they have a cold-water face wash and a stretch outside in the fresh air before they get dressed.

8. They could have the alarm going off half an hour before they need to get up so they have a chance to snuggle down and enjoy being in bed before they have to get up.
9. Get them to have a drink of water before they get up.
10. Tell them that under no circumstances are they to be out of bed before a certain time. Children love doing something safe that they have been forbidden to do.

How you can motivate a child to go to bed at night

Children, just like many of us, hate missing something exciting and they think that as soon as they have gone to bed something exciting and 'unmissable' will happen. They can think it is unfair that other children can stay up longer than them. Some children can feel lonely as they trek off to their room.

Ten tips for making bedtimes bearable
1. Read them a story before bed, in bed.
2. Make their bed feel a special place to them with their choice of pillowcase or soft toys or pictures on the wall.
3. Make sure the activities immediately before bedtime are 'winding down'-type of activities and not hectic, racing around games.
4. Don't give them cola or other fizzy drinks or chocolate or sweets just before bed.
5. Stick to a routine that works.
6. Have gentle music playing or a story tape. Some children prefer the sound of voices and others the sound of music.
7. Get all the preparations done early so they can wander about in their pyjamas for half an hour or so before bed.
8. If they don't get into bed by the time you have said, they should not feel that you must still continue with the rest of the routine, the story and so on, because that could take all night. Children will simply draw out the time further and further beyond your control. If it has got to eight o'clock and that is the time they should be going to sleep, then say they can have the story they

have missed or the talk with you about their day if they get up early in the morning.

9. If they want to stay up to watch something special on TV, set the video instead.

10. Sometimes children need to know why sleep matters. They need to know this is a chance to lie still, clear their mind, and rebuild their energy and strength so that they will enjoy the next day.

13

Home tuition

No one else can motivate our child like we can

When your child is obviously unmotivated at school, you might start to look around for different approaches to schooling. Some parents consider:

- Changing schools
- Tutoring
- Changing class
- Changing seats in the class
- Changing friendship groups
- Withdrawing the child from school altogether

If you are thinking of taking your child out of the school system, there are a great number of issues you will need to look into and think about:

- Who is going to teach your child?
- What is your child going to learn?
- Where is your child going to be taught?
- When is your child going to be taught?

- How are you going to cope with managing your child's learning?
- How is the schooling of your child going to affect family life and the other members of the family?
- How is the schooling of your child going to affect you?

Should I be the teacher?

If you feel that you would be the best teacher for your child, you need to think about your strengths and weaknesses. Think about what you have been involved with in the past.

Are you:

- Someone who gets bored easily?
- Patient?
- Scatty?
- Organised?
- A perfectionist?

Think about your motivation.

The boy who worked better at home than he was working at school

Hayden's parents believed that Hayden could learn far more at home than he could ever learn at school. Hayden loved helping his dad and learning all about science, D.I.Y., building, designing, gardening and cars. He got great pleasure from talking to his mum about the places she had been to, and about the other members of her family who lived a long way away. Hayden was sure they had exotic and exciting lives.

I'm a star, why shouldn't I shine?

Hayden didn't enjoy school. He wished that he could do more of the things he loved at school. He couldn't see why he had to do things which he didn't want to do, so he rarely bothered to do them. His work was erratic. If it was something which fired his imagination, then he would apply himself feverishly, involving everyone else in the family or on his table at school in his efforts. At times like this, he felt that he had star quality and thought that everyone else should agree. While he was the Prima Donna and dictating the pace of what was happening and the way it was happening, he had a lot of energy.

If a teacher or another adult tried to capitalise on his enthusiasm and get him to note something down, to stop talking and to start writing, Hayden would dig his heels in. He thought it should be enough that he had said it. He obviously knew it, and everyone who had heard him would know that he knew it, so what was the point of writing it down?

His writing was very slow and his spelling was very poor, mainly because he missed so many opportunities to have a go at writing and spelling so he didn't get any better. He put all his energy into talking about things, but no energy into writing about them. If the work did not appeal to him, then very little work would be done. He would mess about, getting others into trouble, and would seem confused about what he had to do whenever the teacher tried to prompt him to do a bit more. He would answer questions up to a point, but if the teacher felt they had reached a level of under-standing where he should be able to work on his own, he would say that he really didn't understand what was going on at all.

The showdown

Hayden's teachers explained to his parents that while Hayden had the intellectual ability to do the work, he was not motivated. Hayden's parents found this impossible to believe. Whenever they talked to him about life, he was always fascinated, fascinating, full of information, and brimming with ideas. How could this be a boy who was not motivated?

They felt that the teachers weren't handling Hayden right. They couldn't understand why the teachers couldn't capitalise on his interests and get him to do some work. When they did things with him at home, he often suggested things he could make or try out on his own after their discussions, and frequently busied himself producing pictures, models, cartoons and posters.

Let's try this

At Parents' Evening, the teacher suggested that Hayden needed to do some work over the long summer holiday. Hayden's mum and dad agreed with the teacher that it would be a good idea if Hayden kept a diary of what he had done over the holidays. It would be all about the things that Hayden enjoyed.

Reality check

Over the summer, Hayden's parents' eyes were opened. No matter how they tried to encourage him to write his diary, they couldn't pin him down. He was happy to collect tickets and brochures. He enjoyed visiting museums, playing on the beach, and making models. He started a collection of postcards, but he wouldn't write anything down.

His parents tried lots of ways to motivate Hayden to write. Nothing they did worked. To begin with, they felt that they must be doing something wrong. When they thought about it, they realised that they didn't like doing things that didn't make them feel happy. They had the same problem as Hayden.

They were unhappy when they were nagging Hayden to write; they were bored with the whole project because nothing they suggested was working; they became irritated, and then decided that they weren't going to sacrifice their holiday, so they gave up trying to get Hayden to write his diary. They weren't motivated to keep going with Hayden if he wasn't going to try.

Two weaknesses won't make a strength

It can be a danger when you try and teach your child if both you and your child have the same weakness. It is often the case that when parents try to insist on their children doing something that they are also not very good at, the parents have to work on their own problem before they will be able to get the child to make any progress.

If you are someone who gets bored easily, but you want to teach your child at home yourself, then you will have to set targets and get someone else to monitor those targets so that you are kept focused.

You will also have to resolve the problem of your children refusing to do something that they don't want to do. You can set as many targets as you want, but if your child won't do any work, then that really won't count for anything. You need to decide what you are going to do if trying to teach your child at home isn't working.

Being patient enough to teach

When people watch good teaching, they are always surprised at how much patience is involved. Teaching is no different from any other creative profession. In any creative profession patience is essential because there are so many factors which can influence what you want to happen that you have to be prepared to try something else. You have to work out whether you are achieving what you want and then think what might work next.

Patience is stillness but not emptiness. You are holding yourself ready to choose a skill or a piece of knowledge or spot an opportunity that might work.

The creative part for parents is bringing together things which have been done before in different situations and weaving them in such a way as to help the child make progress.

There are no guarantees that what you have chosen to try will work. When you understand that there is no guaranteed outcome, you will be more patient. You will become impatient if you think that you have put in all the ingredients for success but success has not happened.

Becoming a more patient teacher

Protect the time that you have put aside to teach something. If you try to keep too many activities going at once, you can feel disgruntled and overwhelmed. Focusing your attention on one thing helps you to stay calm and when you are calm you can pay attention. When you pay attention you can see what to do next. When your mind is flitting from one thing to another you can often feel as if you can't get anything done, but when you stop you can get everything done.

Learn as well as teach

Enrol on a course where you have to learn what someone else is teaching you. In this way you will remind yourself of what it is like to be taught. Confusion is a natural part of the early stages of learning any new topic. Careful explanations adjusted to helping you understand more are comforting, encouraging and strengthening. It is always worth running through a checklist before you make any decision about how you are going to teach your child.

Am I too scatty to teach?

Have you been able to get:

- The forms back to school by the date they are needed?
- Your children to school on time?
- To parents' night?
- Your children to pack their bags so that they arrive at school with everything they need for the day?

If you can do all these things then you are not scatty. If you can't do these things you may still not be scatty, you may just have too much on your plate.

Some parents think the freedom to decide when their children will learn, go on holiday, get dressed and so on is so attractive that they take their children out of school. A scatty person will end up with an uneducated child because with no system there are no guidelines for learning and no goalposts to aim for.

Organise yourself

If you do feel you are scatty and you want to teach your child at home, review what you will need.

Get a box of equipment. The equipment must be returned to

that box at the end of the session so that all you have to find for the next session is the box.

Decide what the minimum is that you think you can get away with and what is the maximum you are prepared to do.

Am I too organised to teach?

You can have all the equipment on tap for when the child is ready to seize the moment or you can have decided ahead of time what your child is going to learn and feel very offended when they don't.

You can have a loose plan, which means you can take different opportunities depending on what seems sensible at the time, or you can have a plan that is so loosely constructed that it is difficult to put into operation when it is needed.

Some people who think that they are organised are only able to cope if everyone around them behaves the way they need them to. Parents who have had successful work lives can find themselves completely at sea when trying to cope with their small children.

Routines which have been constructed at work to make sure the day goes efficiently are much more difficult to construct in a family, particularly if children are strong-willed or live in a world of their own or don't get on with other members of the family.

You win some, you lose some

Deborah was always aware of what the museums had to offer and when she rang the museum about their new educational pack and tour on 'Creatures of the Sea', she had no doubt that her two children – John, nine, and Felicity, seven – would enjoy every minute of it. When the pack arrived through the post, she was delighted with the two workbooks that had been included. They were excellent; full of interesting questions and activities. Deborah decided that on Monday they could go to the museum and then each morning for the rest of the week they could have great fun completing the workbooks. She felt that when the books were finished the children would be really pleased with what they had done and know a lot about creatures of the sea.

The visit
Monday came and the threesome set off for the museum bristling with sharp pencils and notepads. The first hiccup came when there was an argument over who was going to carry the bag with the sandwiches. John didn't want to and Felicity swung the bag around hitting John with it 'accidentally'. The next little incident was over who could sit by the window. There was much elbowing and grunting while Deborah tried to rise above it all, smiling and speaking quietly and looking forward to getting to the museum where she was sure things would improve.

The row
John and Felicity hardly noticed when they got to the museum because they were now in a world of bad tempers and bickering. They met up with the museum guide who was going to show them round. Deborah set a wonderful example of how to listen but the children behaved as if everything that was being said and everything that was in the museum was boring beyond belief.

Deborah marvelled at the museum guide's ability to carry on and remain so affable in the face of such disdain. The exhibits really were fascinating and the guide had so much to say which was interesting, intriguing and informative.

It will be OK when we get home
Deborah was optimistic that, in spite of appearances, the children really would have learned something from their trip. She certainly had. There had been other times where the children had seemed uninterested yet after the event had been full of what they had seen, heard and done.

Unfortunately this time this was not the case. When Deborah got out the workbooks the next day, John and Felicity just looked blank. They couldn't remember anything they had seen or anything the museum guide had said.

Deborah began to wonder whether she had dreamt it all.

Lower your expectations

In real life not everything you do works out the way you had hoped, planned or anticipated. When the energy is there you can get learning out of almost nothing. When the energy isn't there you are unlikely to feel satisfied with what has happened. However, sometimes what appears to have been the most unsatisfactory event can reveal ways of doing something better next time.

How do you know if you are on the right track?

It can be much more difficult to know that you have done something successfully when you are home-schooling than it is at work. At work there are benchmarks by which you can judge your progress and even if everything else is going wrong the pay-cheque still comes in. At home it is much more unpredictable and difficult to assess which part of your effort is worth carrying on with and what you need to change and there is no pay-cheque.

You can't tell what you are going to be like until you actually do it but it is always worth having a fall-back position if your decision to home-school proves unworkable.

14

Rewards, bribes and incentives

Questions parents ask themselves

Parents may ask themselves:

- Should I ever give money?
- If I have given a reward to one child must I give a reward to all the others for doing the same thing?
- Are sweets a good reward?
- What should I do if I have rewarded a child for something and then found out that they got someone else to do the task for them?
- If I start off by rewarding something then should I always reward the child for doing the same thing?
- Who should decide on the reward?
- Is it reasonable to give a reward because it suits me to get the job done or have a break?
- Should I reward other people's children?
- If I give a reward am I doing more damage?
- Are rewards really bribes?

- Are rewards always bad?
- What is the difference between a reward and a bribe?
- If I give a reward is it going to be a good lesson for how life really works?
- Do children who get rewards end up being spoilt?

Rewards, bribes and incentives

Rewards, bribes and incentives for you – not a problem

How do you get on track, stay on track or get yourself back on track? The chances are that you are happy to give yourself rewards, bribes and incentives.

Rewards, bribes and incentives for your children – what a problem

This is an area fraught with difficulty. Parents can disagree with each other. They can disagree with friends. They can disagree with grandparents.

Parents plan and plot ways to motivate their children. They might use what their own parents found worked with them. They use what they see, hear or read has worked for other people. They hope they can use rewards in a sensible way so that their family life is trouble-free and runs smoothly.

Parents have to feel in control of the rewards, bribes and incentives they use with their children.

One of the difficulties is that what one person sees as a bribe is seen as a reward by someone else. What one person can see as an incentive can be seen as a punishment or bribe by someone else.

The word 'bribe' is emotive for many parents. They would never think of giving their child a bribe. They give incentives. They would never use the word 'bribe' because they are trying to achieve something else with an incentive. They might use incentives which other people would think could just as easily be called bribes.

Often the words bribe, incentive or reward are interchangeable, and it is a matter of choice which word is used. Sometimes there are clear differences between the way families see what they are doing. One family is comfortable with the idea of focusing on the reward or bribe. The other is comfortable focusing on the incentive that led to the effort to achieve the goal.

Rewards, bribes and incentives should all have a positive effect on children's progress. They can all have their place. In an ideal world they will be used at the right time to fit a particular situation and to fit a particular child.

A public matter

Some parents are relaxed about how they motivate their children. They have no worries that what they have chosen to do is right. They are happy to talk to anyone about what methods they use, how they have worked and what they might do next time.

A private matter

Some parents can feel rewards are a dangerous thing even to talk about with their friends. Letting friends know what rewards they resort to with their children can feel like they are washing their dirty linen in public.

Even worse for some parents is that they can feel they are revealing that their own children are manipulating them. Parents are worried that the rewards they have decided on might reveal some peculiarity in them to other people.

They may be made to feel their child's not normal because their child needs a reward in this situation, or they may feel that they are out of control because other people don't seem to need rewards to get their children to do what they have to do.

The truth is that there are few parents who don't use rewards and there are few parents who don't worry about the impact their rewards might have on the progress of their children.

Confused thinking

One of the problems about rewards, bribes and incentives is that adults themselves can be confused about what it is they are doing:

- Is saying the child can have 20 pence if he gets all his spellings right a bribe or a reward?
- Is giving £10 per 'A' at GCSE a bribe, reward or incentive?
- What is giving a bike to a child who has passed an entrance exam?
- Is washing the family car something the children should do because they get paid for it or do because they are a member of the family?

Parental choice
Children are developing all of the time and keeping up with how they are thinking at every moment is impossible. Parents will be relaxed about rewards if they are ready to adjust to what motivates their children at the moment.

The most important thing is that parents feel comfortable about the choices they make and the offers they give to their children. They need to understand why they feel a reward is necessary.

How do you decide when to reward?
Is it when:

- Your children are only doing it because you say that they have to?
- It is something that your children just have to do and no one would find it pleasant?
- Other parents are giving their children a reward?
- You got a reward when you were a child for doing a similar thing?

Clear thinking – the principle should be progress
When you let your children know in advance that they will get a treat for doing something special you are hoping they:

- Realise you respect their effort
- Work harder than they perhaps would otherwise
- Prioritise something that you think is important

The progress that you are hoping for is that your child will start to respect *his own* efforts, realise that he can change how hard *he* works and prioritise what *he* thinks is important.

You hope that the sense of achievement he gets will become his reward in the future.

Showing approval

By giving a reward you are showing approval because your child has:

- Finished
- Got started
- Tried hard
- Been brave
- Been sensible
- Had a go
- Kept going
- Been kind
- Been thoughtful

The progress that you are hoping for is that your children will continue to do the things that get approval. Your children will feel redefined as people who can rise to an occasion. Knowing they have achieved something that other people have noticed and felt worthy of rewarding means that they will be confident that other things they do can be valued as well. They will be motivated to stretch themselves so they take on responsibilities and challenges whether there is a reward or not.

A word of warning

We all like to give food as a reward or treat but rewarding with food is becoming a real problem because some children:

- Eat so much sugary food as part of their daily diet that they don't have enough substantial food to absorb the sugar in the treat. They become hyperactive, wilful, miserable and aggressive

- Are affected by foods which don't affect other children. A meal covered in tomato sauce can be an incendiary device for some children
- Find concentrated fruit juices or fizzy drinks difficult to process. They are agitated after a drink and find it hard to behave reasonably
- Don't eat enough non-processed food to cope with the demands of highly processed treats

If you find your child behaves well sometimes and terribly at other times, keep a check on what they are eating. Keep a food diary. If they have a good day note what they have eaten. If they have a bad day note it as well. Don't assume that a food which works well for one person works well for everyone.

15

Letting go

Relax and gain strength, confidence and motivation

The importance of knowing how to relax is accepted by most people.

In families it is very important that the adults understand how to let their anxieties go for their own mental health and the mental health of their children. It is also important that children learn how to relax.

Relaxation is the state when we are detached from the anxieties and preoccupations that can keep all of us stuck in a rut. Relaxation liberates everyone so they can find new ways to move forward in their own lives. We let go of the old and have space for the new.

Letting go

When you are trying to motivate someone to do something you are often very focused on what you think they should do and how you are going to be able to get them to do it. You can trap yourself in one position where you can only think one thought.

If you are so focused on what you expect to happen and how you expect it to happen, you might miss something which would have made finding the right motivation easier.

People often think that letting go is the same as giving up. But if you can learn how to let go for a short time, or let go of what is unhelpful without feeling the need to give up, you will find life much easier. Other people will be more prepared to listen and you will be prepared to hear.

Letting go means taking a break from the thoughts that are whirling around in your head. It means slowing your pace down. It means allowing your common sense to surface.

Most of us know how to let go and calm down but we just don't do it enough. We throw ourselves at problems or keep chasing after difficulties until either the problem disappears or we run out of energy. We only look for the difficulties and we keep an eye open all the time for problems. It is far better if we can give ourselves lots of chances to recover a balance between what is working and what we still need to sort out. Letting go means we can find the space and the time to see what is working and we get better at recognising what is working and why it is working.

How to let go

You can read this to yourself and do one bit at a time. You can read it all and do what you remember. You can read it to your children. Just reading the words will help. Practising will be even better. It is your choice. You can be tense and in the doldrums or in conflict or you can be at ease and aware of the way forward.

- *Breathe in through your nose and then slowly and steadily breathe out through your mouth. Keep your breathing deep and steady.*
- *Tighten your toes by curling them over — and then let them go.*
- *Tighten your feet by curling them up — and then let them go.*
- *Tighten your legs by making them go stiff — and then let them go.*
- *Tighten your bottom, squeeze it together — and then let it go.*
- *Tighten your tummy by pulling it in as tight as you can — and then let it go.*
- *Tighten your back — and then let it go.*
- *Tighten your chest — and then let it go.*

- *Tighten your fists, squeeze them together into two tight fists – and then let them go.*
- *Tighten your arms by making them go stiff – and then let them go.*
- *Hunch your shoulders up to your ears – and then let them go.*
- *Squeeze your face into a tight ball – and then let it go.*
- *Lift your eyebrows up towards your hair – and then let them go.*

Relaxing with your family will help. You can read your children's picture books to them, to yourself, or to your partner or friend. You can do some colouring in. You can work with plasticine. Just take time away from wanting to make something happen or wanting to do something or see it being done. Just be and see how powerful just being can be.

Some stories to give your imagination some exercise

Twinkle, twinkle little star

Imagine yourself sitting on a bench in a park. It is quite a windy day and every so often some leaves which have fallen from the trees nearby are blown by your feet. Your attention is caught by the way they swirl and curl.

Further up the path you spot a brown paper bag being blown along the ground by the breeze. This bag is intriguing because it seems to be empty, the way it is being swept along the ground, and yet it looks as though the bag has something in it.

You get up with a smile playing on your lips and stop the bag with your foot as it gets level with you. You bend down and pick up the bag. It keeps its shape as though it is full of something but it is as light as a feather.

You open the bag feeling strangely excited and interested to see what is inside. When you look in the bag at first you just see deep, deep black. Then in the corner of the bag you spot something twinkling. In the bag you have a piece of the midnight sky. It is a dark, inky black and there, sparkling in the darkness, is a bright star. You marvel at what you see.

You shut the bag gently and when you open it again you wonder whether the magic inside will have disappeared. You are thrilled when you peep inside the bag again and you spot the star glimmering in the jet-black sky, still inside the bag.

This is your own special bag of magic. You keep it with you. You can fold it small. No matter where you are or what time it is or what has happened, whenever you remember to look inside your magic bag you will be able to spot the glittering star.

History is part of me and I am part of history

Imagine that it is getting towards the end of the afternoon and you find yourself walking along a path that you often use to get home. Further ahead at the side of the path you can see a figure sitting hunched over a little campfire.

The person is cooking something in a pot over the fire. You smell the tasty, savoury aroma of a stew bubbling over the flames. As you get closer, you can see the face of the person who is by the fire. It is an old, old face. This person looks as old as time. Their face and hands are wrinkled but not frightening. They look wise and knowing, as if they have seen and been through many things. They make a space for you to sit down next to them on the log. As you sit down you notice something about the person's coat.

It is a big coat, a long coat with many pockets. Something is happening on the coat. The coat is like a screen that can show pictures. As you stare at the coat, you see scenes from history being played out on different parts of the coat. You see travellers visiting places that no one has visited before. You see a battle on one of the pockets. You see pyramids being built on another pocket. Across the back, you see astronauts waving a flag as they stand on the moon. All over the coat you see events from history. Things from history that you have read about, heard about and learned about.

The ancient person pulls something from deep inside one of the coat pockets. It looks like a big ice cube. The wise one hands it to you. You take it and as you do you realise that it is not ice but a glass cube. You look into the cube and see something moving. You look with amazement. You realise that inside the glass you can see other events taking place but these events are from your own history. You see yourself learning to walk and to ride a bike. You see your first day at school and a birthday party when you were little. You smile as you see the person you were learning to do things you find so easy to do now.

It is time to leave. You say goodbye to the old person and carry on walking home. Every now and then you take the glass cube from your pocket and look into it. You are reminded of things in your past. You see yourself meeting an old friend for the first time. You see yourself going on a trip, playing a game, laughing with people you like and love. Any time you remember, you can see history and see how wonderful the world can be.

Stretching, rolling, thinking and creating

Picture yourself sitting at a table. In front of you on the table you have a large lump of clay. When you reach out and touch it, it feels hard and cold. You try to mould it but it is hard because the clay is so solid. You press and pull at the clay to make it softer. It takes a long time but gradually the clay softens and warms up. You keep kneading the clay, rolling it, stretching it and pushing it. Eventually the clay is flexible enough to start shaping it into a bowl. You mould it around your fist using your fingers and thumbs to get the clay thinner at the edges. You keep working on the pot, shaping it until you have it just the way you want. Now looking at it on the table in front of you, you find it hard to remember the cold and solid lump that you started off with. You have changed its shape and how it feels. You have transformed it. Now the bowl can be baked hard in a kiln and decorated with colourful glazes. The bowl can be used to hold small objects. It has become something that can be practical at the same time as pretty.

Lift-off

Imagine, in your mind's eye, your favourite meal. Picture it there on the plate or in a bowl. Is it hot with steam coming off it, or is it cold? Imagine the colours of the food and the shapes the food makes on the plate.

Now imagine a clear balloon forming around that dish of your favourite food. Dangling from the bottom of the balloon is a string. Grab hold of that string and you will feel the tiniest tug on your arm as the balloon tries to lift you off your feet. Keep holding on to the balloon and now imagine your favourite place. Picture it in your mind's eye. It might be an indoor place or it might be an outdoor place. What is in the place? What are the colours and the textures in the place? Is the place somewhere you go to a lot, or is it somewhere you have only been to one or two times? Perhaps it is somewhere that you love reading and hearing about but you haven't been there yet. Now imagine a clear balloon forming around the picture of the place. You can still see the place inside the balloon.

There is a string dangling down from the balloon and you add that string to the one in your hand. Now the two balloons can almost lift you off your feet.

The next picture you are going to imagine in your mind's eye is the picture of a piece of work that you have done that you were really proud of. Perhaps it is a story you wrote. It could be a maths sheet that you were really pleased with because you did much better on it than normal. Maybe it is a picture that you took a long time over. It could be an essay or a model you constructed. It could be a difficult book that you managed to read from beginning to end. Once you have the picture in your mind's eye, think of a clear balloon forming around the picture. That balloon has a piece of string as well so now you have three balloons.

These three balloons can lift you right off your feet. They can carry you over anything that gets in your way. They can lift you over buildings and across roads. They can take you over mountains and seas. They can get you across wide spaces and over tall objects. When you want to come back down to land, you just let go of the strings and you will float gently down to the ground. If you need the help of the balloons again you find that the strings dangle down just near enough to you for you to be able to grab them. With these three balloons you can get to wherever you want to be.

Motivation and Family Groups

For some years we have been very impressed by the quality of support, care and empowerment available to parents in the Wirral and Chester area that is provided by Family Groups.

Family Groups are made up of six to eight parents who can make friendships, build trust and find ways to cope with the burdens and joys of parenthood. Parents are given the chance to learn skills to help them help their children.

Parents and children who belong to these groups become motivated. They want to develop their potential. They feel supported and strengthened through belonging to a family group.

For more information about Family Groups in your area, ask local churches, health visitors, doctors, teachers or social workers, or ask at your local library.

For more information about the Wirral and Chester Family Groups, contact:

The Catholic Children's Society
St Paul's House
Farmfield Drive, Beechwood, Prenton, Wirral CH43 7ZT

Index

anxiety 58–9, 60–1, 62–4
apathy 31–2, 102
approval, need for 34
attention 144
avoidance 153–4

babies 2, 84
bad habits 75–6
ball games, playing safely 85–6
bedtime 182–3
behaviour 79–81, 93
bitchiness 167–8
book reviews 26–7
boredom 11, 15–16
boys, not listening to mothers
    141–3
bribes 194–6
bright children, demotivation of 12
bullying 166–7

caring 91
change 141, 143–5
checklists 157

clues, listening out for 89, 90
commands 142–3
comments, upsetting 164–5
communication 119–21, 143
competition 30
comprehension 25–6
concentration, lack of 131
confidence, loss of after illness
    42–5, 65
    in logic 47–8
    and loss of optimism 50–1
    and maturity 48–9
    in memory 46–7
    rebuilding imagination 52–3
consideration for others 176–8
contribution to groups 35, 38–9,
    93
credibility 157
crises 118
    talking about 119–21

daydreams 50
demotivation 6–7, 12, 31, 145

depression 9, 16–18, 102, 103
diet 55
difference, enjoyment of 73, 75, 77, 80
disappointments 105
    coping with 106–9
distractions 131–2

eating 55, 180–1, 197–8
education 12, 13
emotions 104, 164
    expressing 119
enthusiasm, loss of 41–2
essay writing 27–9
exams, fear of 21, 44
excuses 74
exercise 55
explanations, to help children cope 96–100
eye contact 89, 172

failure, fear of 19–20, 60–1
fair play 86, 95
fallback positions 112, 113
families
    different standards of behaviour 79–81
    problems in 36–7, 54, 80, 116–17, 118
fear of getting it wrong 19–20
following up 95
food *see* eating
friends 33, 50, 80–1, 94
    making 174–5
frustration 12
full marks 157

getting it wrong 19–20
getting up 181–2

giving up 111–23
groups
    being passive member 163
    involvement in 35, 38–9, 87–95
growing up 83–4, 86–7

habits 75–6
having a go 30–40
helpfulness 90
home tuition 184–92
homework 10–11, 25, 77, 112, 114–16
    distraction from 131–2
    improving 157
    making interesting 13–15
    parents' support with 125–33, 134–5, 136–40, 147–8
    in rough 155, 156, 157, 158
    too busy for 125–6, 127

illness, and loss of confidence 42–8, 65
imagination 52–3, 201–5
improvements 17–18
'in crowd' 168–9
incentives 194–6
independent, becoming 79
information 151, 152
instructions 154
interest/s 109
    finding 15–16
    losing 103
    others taking, in children 33
interference, timing of 144–5
involvement 87–95

jealousy 34
jigsaws 47–8, 117

209

keywords 28
knowing yourself 108–9, 110
knowledge, framework of 152–3

learning 20, 66, 69–70
    by mistakes 158–9
    stress caused by 20–2
letting go 199–201
listening 92
logic, loss of confidence in 47–8
long-term view 150, 151–2
losing, coping with 179–80
loyalty 91

maturity 48–9, 86, 87
memory, loss of confidence in
    46–7
mistakes 20, 29, 66, 131, 132
    learning by 158–9
motivation
    adult 3–6
    maintaining 7–8, 12

needs of others, recognising 91,
    176–8
nightmares 50
'no', saying 140
no good, thinking yourself to be
    57–70
notes 28
noticing 90, 92, 153

observation 88, 153
opportunities for doing things
    136–40
optimism 50–1, 55
options, closing off 154
organisational skills 79, 149
    for homework 155–9

others
    consideration for 91, 176–8
    valuing 93–4
outsiders 169

pace, working out 90, 156
parents
    beliefs about children 126–7
    doing homework 125–33,
        134–5, 136–40, 147–8
    not in control 120, 122
    reassurance for 60
    strategies for staying sane
        63–4
    wanting children to be like
        them 135–6
patience 49–50, 188–9
perfect copies 159
planning 140–1
politeness 175–6
praise 38, 98–9, 129, 130
proactive role 108

relaxation 199, 200–1
responsibility 39, 83, 90
reward 4, 7–8, 193–7
role models 38

sadness 16–17

safety 83, 84
    at play 85–6
saying no 140
school, problems at 34, 61, 103,
    114, 169–70, 185–7
    avoidance of school 22, 58–9
    changing schools 71–7
    underperforming 31–2, 65–6,
        73, 74–5

self-doubt 165, 167
selfishness 34, 85
self-reliance 116
setbacks 108, 113
sharing 91, 173–4
shyness 36–8, 172–3
siblings 32–3
social skills 160–1, 165–83
  teaching 161–4
sorting things out 112, 113, 114–16
space, giving people 94
spelling lists 13–15
spontaneity 140–1
staleness 132–3
stammering 171
stillness 88, 132, 163
stimulation 15
stories
  learning from 151
  writing 23–9
stress 129–30
  caused by learning 20–2
stupidity, feelings of 20
support 114–16, 118, 147–8, 172
swots 169–70
sympathy 118

teachers 66–7, 69–70, 75
  bad teaching experiences 68–9

good teaching experiences
  67–8
teaching
  at home 188–92
  patience for 188–9
teamwork 147–8
time 143–4
  blocks of 140–1
  giving people 94
tiredness 44, 125
trial runs 155
turn-taking 178–9
tutors 133–5

underperformance 31–2, 65–6,
  73, 74–5
unhappiness, coping with 103–4

valuing other people 93–4
valuing yourself 165–71
visualisation 52–3

willingness 53–4
workbooks 11–12
writing 23–9
  feeling scared about 22

zest for life 41–2, 56
  loss of 42–5, 54–6